Positioned *for the* Exchange
Who Will *Impact* the Next Generation?

Dr. René Rochester

WINEPRESS WP PUBLISHING

ISBN 1-57921-447-9
Library of Congress Catalog Card Number: 2002100044

⚘ Acknowledgements

I would first like to give honor where honor is due, to my Heavenly Father and Lord and Savior Jesus Christ. He is ever so faithful. The completion of this book is nothing less of a miracle. For years my heart has been filled with a longing to encourage those who also have a passion for this generation of youth. As a former high school coach, I found great joy when my team would recognize they had within them the basic skills and ability to improvise if their opponent took away an option. Their foundational skills would surface and a poised decision was made. I want to take this time to thank those who have instilled in me the foundational skills and have been used to shape me into who I am today. First and foremost to my mother Bernice R. Bates who knows me, because she had me. I am living out much of what was instilled in me as a little girl. I am grateful for you. My sisters Karen and Patricia, the formative years as children the laughter and fussing to the current day reminding each other from whence we came. Thank you for believing in me and encouraging me to press forward. My fifth and sixth grade teacher, Sue Mcglinn, you saw the hidden potential while I was fighting on the playground of Ashfield Elementary School. From fifth grade to the present you have been a friend and encouragement. Carmella D. Hull for the countless hours you have served me with an unselfish heart in the midst of your own pain and were a friend to me when I wasn't very friendly. Thank you for seeing the vision in my heart and designing the PHAT STAR model. How can I say enough for the prayers, scriptures of encouragement, your business mind, typing of the references, and just the day-to-day press? I am so thankful for you. Dr. Claudette Copeland, (Pastor "C") thank you for your continual encouragement and gracious manner of dealing with the hidden issues of my heart and willing to pour the balm of Gilead on the wounded places. Truly you are one with a shepherd's heart. Bishop Copeland a true visionary! I am grateful for the "coach" I see in you. Thank you for believing and investing in what The Father has deposited in me. Urban SET partners I am so grateful for your prayers and encouragement. Peg and John thanks for your continual support. Bruce and Chris your daily prayers for me have at many times carried me when I felt crippled in my own soul. Darlene and Ray, I am a witness of how your lives have blossomed. Thanks for your love, prayers and encouragement. Women of UCW, thank you for your prayers, to Deborah, Mother, Junias and Ashley thanks for your prayers. Latricia and Anthony thanks for your believing in PHAT STAR and allowing us to pilot the program in Michigan. All of you who participated in the PHAT STAR WORKSHOPS and intensive training thank you for making it possible. Dr. Norvell Northcutt and Dr. Robert L. Marion thank you for believing in what was placed in me and pushing me toward excellence while hearing the heart of the PHAT STAR message, to empower people. Your position on my dissertation committee was handpicked of The Lord! Dr. Gottlieb and Steinhardt thank you for hanging in there to see the evidence. Dr. Peterson, what can I say? You are now on the PHAT STAR team, and a true player!! Thank you for steering the dissertation committee and stirring my heart to persevere. To my new Community Bible Study friends, thank you for your intercession. Anita you have been appointed for such a time as this! Your words and prayers have been used to push me through some of the stuck places. Celina, the words spoken on the plane that day were ordained of The Lord! You were used to bring much clarity that day to the hidden fears of writing! Thank you for speaking what you saw with grace and confidence. To WinePress Publishing, thank you for the opportunity.

Finally, in a book, what I have watched for over 12 years! Dr. René Rochester's powerful, effective, Christ centered teaching on mentoring and disciple making. I have seen literally thousands impacted for a lifetime by this awesome woman of God! Now everyone can see on paper what God has put inside the heart of His messenger for this generation of young people!

—Stephan Moore
Assistant Executive Director
Kids Across America

Contents

Preface: What is a Relay Race? ix
Introduction: Understanding the Race xi

Part One: The Theoretical Underpinning of
PHAT STAR EDUCATION

1. Basic Rules of the Baton Exchange 17
2. An Ecological Perspective of
   Adolescent Risk Taking 27
3. The Macro-System: Socio-Economic Status
   and the Adolescent 37
4. Cultural Diversity and Multicultural Education 41

Part Two: United to Rebuild and Restore

5. The Call to Collaboration 55
6. Times, Trends and Teens 61
7. Media Coverage and Its Impact....................................... 71
8. Prepared for the Exchange 81
9. Awakening the Church to Community
   Intervention 87
10. The School Educator and Parent Collaboration 95

Positioned for the Exchange

11. The "STAR" Model 99
12. A Welcomed Witness "What Has Been Said" 105

Bibliography 111

~ PREFACE

What is a Relay Race?

I n 1996, I can remember sitting in the stands in Atlanta, Georgia with my mother hearing the cheers of thousands as the United States men's four by one hundred meter relay had begun. People were cheering "USA" "USA". The thought going through my mind as the first runner turned the curve was: "I hope they have a good handoff." To be positioned for a clean baton exchange is usually what determines who will win the race.

A relay team consists of four participants. The first runner carries a baton about 30 centimeters long. After running a certain distance, called a leg, the athlete hands the baton to the next team member. The exchange must occur within a zone 20 meters long. If the runners do not exchange the baton within this zone, their team is disqualified. In some meets there are medley relays where each athlete runs a different distance. The passing of the baton is where the race is won or lost. Both the incoming and outgoing runner must be positioned for the transition while staying in the exchange zone. In reference to education we must ask ourselves: "Are we prepared and positioned to make a successful transition of information and impartation of character to the next generation?" Generational impartation is similar to passing the baton in

Positioned for the Exchange

a relay race we must know our position on the team, and be willing to handle the baton responsibly.

As a runner at the University of Texas at Austin, I had great anticipation to compete in the four by four hundred meter relay. At any given meet based on the weather conditions or the design of the track (long or short curves and short or long straight-a-ways) our coach would have us run different legs of the race. The athlete with acceleration out of the starting blocks, who ran curves well, would run the first or third leg of the race. If the straight-a-way was long on the backstretch, and weather conditions were windy, the runner with a good amount of stamina and muscle density would run that leg. Our position had much to do with our preparation and individual body composition. However, the most important part of the relay was the exchange of the baton. A smooth transition usually meant a faster time, a possible medal or winning the race.

In most cases, the baton exchange is where a relay race is won or lost. When the incoming runner is positioned for the exchange, the outgoing runner would eye a familiar mark identified on the track (we called this the fly zone). Numerous drills equipped a runner to judge the marking of the fly zone. The mark was placed by the outgoing runner having judged the incoming speed of their teammate. The incoming runner would run their leg not slowing until they had passed the identified mark. At that moment, the outgoing runner would explode and accelerate from their ready position. The ideal transition would take place if, on command of the incoming runner, a steady hand would stretch back and grip the baton and never lose stride. When the incoming runner felt a good exchange, they would finish in their lane and cheer their teammate on! Hopefully at the close of this book, you too will be prepared for a smooth transition to the next generation. Imparting an inheritance of knowledge and value, cheering the outgoing runner on to the finish line!

⚡ Introduction

Understanding the Race

The day our high school coach informed us of who would run the four by one hundred meter relay he sat us down and explained the purpose of the race. We were told about the team's former accolades and the current conditions in the league. We learned about the other relay teams and what it would take to beat them. Finally coach would address our individual potential and assure us he would do his best to tap any dormant ability while refining our skills. We have an opportunity to coach a generation of youth speaking to their untapped ability and empowering them to a wholesome future.

In *The Handbook of Adolescent Health Risk Behavior*, Sells and Blum state:

> We have two decades of research and literature on those factors associated with positive outcomes among youth raised in high-risk social environments. If, over the next decade, we choose to build programs that enhance resilience among youth at highest risk for negative outcomes, then we have a chance when next these data are compiled to see trends in the social morbidities, homicide and suicide that are akin to what we see here for motor vehicle deaths—a dramatic reduction. If

on the other hand, we are paralyzed by the myth that "nothing can be done," then we stand a great likelihood of living out that self-fulfilling prophecy. (Sells, & Blum, 1996, p.29)

Educators, parents and concerned adults for the next generation, must know that something can be done. Each of us has a role in empowering youth to abstain from decisions that could lead to their morbidity and mortality. As our nation takes on a greater diverse complexion, there has come a need for models that would address today's society. Preventive Holistic Adolescent Training: Saving Teens At Risk (PHAT STAR) Education is a multicultural holistic design fitting for the diverse communities of our nation.

The Carnegie Council asks a broad question to those who work with at-risk youth: "Can we envision how the basic institutions of society—families, schools, churches, youth organizations, health care agencies, and the media—buttressed by powerful sectors like higher education, the scientific community, and government, might cooperate in meeting the developmental needs of youth?" (Carnegie Council, 1997, p.1)

Education psychologists associate development and maturity with *puberty* or *adolescence,* a period of life known as a transition of accelerating physical, psychological, social, cultural and cognitive development. Only by understanding the myriad of psychological, sociological and cultural influences on adolescent risk behavior can we begin to meet the challenges posed by risks behaviors, and design the necessary programs and curricula to prevent and reduce risk. For example, many of us desire a better understanding of transitional developmental issues leading to unhealthy behavioral patterns such as relationship choices, which become sexual in contact. There are numerous perceptions of what is meant by *sexual contact.* Rather than argue about which boundaries of contact are proper; it makes more sense to address them as progressions of potential risk in physical relationships. A section of this book will introduce parents, mentors, teachers and clergy to effective ways to teach wholeness in relationships to a diverse community of youth. A desired purpose is to alleviate sensitivity constraints, while communicating a message of wholeness, responsible communication and contact in relationships.

The focus of this book is to encourage, educate and empower adults and adolescents willing to impact future generations with vision and possibility. We can be positioned to pass on knowledge and wisdom, while creating possibilities for production and construction of that knowledge.

PART ONE

The Theoretical Underpinning of
PHAT STAR EDUCATION

If there is no foundation how do we build?

~ Chapter 1

Basic Rules of the Baton Exchange

Adult Learning / PHAT STAR Adult Workshops

Everyone who participates on the relay understands the philosophy, or general principle of a baton exchange. For example, our coach not only worked on drills with us, but also explained to us the rationale of how each runner should be positioned in the lane. The first athlete would run on the inside of the lane encouraged to lean into the curve and make the exchange to the second athlete who ran on the outside of the lane, this gave the runners an opportunity to use the width of the lane for a smooth exchange. Each athlete would alternate inside to out side until the final runner. This foundational rule was adhered to every time we would compete.

Preventive Holistic Adolescent Training: Saving Teens at Risk (PHAT STAR) has a theoretical underpinning with general field-tested principles used throughout all training and curriculum. PHAT STAR began as an intervention program designed by myself Dr. René Rochester as my dissertation thesis (Rochester, 1999). The individuals who participated in the intervention program were inner city youth workers, educators and lay ministers from diverse backgrounds. The goal of the training was to imbue the youth workers with knowledge and understanding of an ecological model of prevention that is developmentally, and culturally appropriate. The program content addressed sexual behavioral patterns leading to pregnancy, sexually transmitted infections and disease, substance abuse and violence prevention. The theoretical foundation of the program intervened on known psychological, sociological and theological mediating mechanisms that account for some of the behaviors demonstrated amongst today's youth culture.

The PHAT STAR philosophy was designed to work with key stakeholders in the community who are willing to collaborate with the education department. The rationale being youth spend most of their day in school. A holistic community based program allows for a broad range of strategies and curriculum formats. In this design holistic education refers to understanding the whole person—body, soul and spirit and how these three constructs interact in our external behavior. New definitions of behavior have blurred the lines between behaviorism and cognitive psychology. For many years behavioral approaches have ignored the power and vitality of the inner life of students and their capacity to create personally and intellectually relevant meanings. A holistic concept provides the instructor, no matter the institution of education, (family, school, church etc. . . .) a comprehensive strategy of teaching youth preventive health measures and promoting wellness. As concerned adults we should position ourselves to prepare young people for the real world. When youth know what will be expected of them, and have an understanding of the basic issues of life, it enhances their ability to stand up under pressures and make informed decisions that could save their lives. The theoretical underpinning of PHAT STAR Education is: adult learning, ecological models and theories of adolescent risk-taking behavior, postmodern curriculum development, multicultural education and the church as a nurturing community.

Community Hosted Adult Workshops
The PHAT STAR adult workshop training and curriculum are associated with Malcolm Knowles, a leading researcher in

the area of adult education believes that learning is a social activity and adults learn better when they interact with other people (Knowles, 1973). Some of the andragogical goals of the PHAT STAR philosophy are to provide collaborative opportunities for educators, parents, clergy and community youth workers to be encouraged. The workshops emphasize core issues pertaining to family, culture and community. This design provides an authentic assessment process actively involving adult youth workers, educators and parents in activities joining objectives, methodologies and measurement. According to Knowles, in order for adult education to fulfill its mission effectively in the world of the future, the clientele it receives must be innovative and self-directed learners. For this result to be accomplished requires a major restructuring of the educational enterprise around the concept of lifelong learning, including a restructuring of the roles of teachers (Knowles, 1984).

With the demographic trends and developments related to the nation's changing ethnicity and future workforce, there appears to be a need for restructuring educational curricula in order to prepare the workforce needed for tomorrow. Andragogy was derived from the Greek words *aner*, meaning literally "man, not boy," and *agogous* (leader of) which had been coined by a German educator in 1833, and was defined as the art and science of helping adults to learn. (Knowles, 1978) Throughout the years the students of Malcolm Knowles have used his adragogical model of adult education and put it to work in all kinds of organizations both in the United States and abroad. In his book *Adragogy in Action,* he lists five assumptions of the adult learner:

1. The concept of the learner,
2. The role of the learner's experience,
3. Readiness to learn,
4. Orientation to learning,
5. Motivation to learn.

19

Positioned for the Exchange

Edward C. Lindeman laid the foundation for a systematic theory about adult learning. He believed the approach to adult education would be through the route of situations, not subjects. According to Lindeman our academic system has grown in reverse order. In conventional education the student is required to adjust himself to an established curriculum; in adult education the curriculum is built around student's needs and interests. An adult finds himself in specific situations with respect to his work, his recreation, his family-life, his community-life, etcetera—situations that call for adjustments (Lindeman, 1926). The PHAT STAR adult workshop model is built around the needs and interests of adults working with adolescents. Lindeman describes the highest value in adult education as the learner's experience. He encourages small group activities where aspiring adults who desire to keep their minds fresh and vigorous can begin to learn by confronting pertinent situations. These are the ones who dig down into the reservoirs of their experience before resorting to texts and secondary facts. The PHAT STAR adult workshop allows the youth workers to be led in discussions by their peers, who are also seeking after wisdom and not oracles; this according to Lindeman constitutes the setting for adult education, the modern quest for life's meaning (Lindeman, 1926).

Lindeman speaks of adult education as an attempt to discover a new method and create a new incentive for learning; its implications are qualitative, not quantitative. Lindeman, the pioneering theorist, identifies several key assumptions about adult learners that have been supported by later research and that established some foundational stones of modern adult theory:

1. Adults are motivated to learn as they experience needs and interests that learning will satisfy; therefore, these are the appropriate starting points for organizing adult learning activities.
2. Adults' orientation to learning is life-centered; therefore the appropriate units for organizing adult learning are life situations, not subjects.

3. Experience is the richest resource for adults' learning; therefore, the core methodology of adult education is the analysis of experience.

4. Adults have a deep need to be self-directing; therefore, the role of the teacher is to engage in a process of mutual inquiry with them rather than to transmit his or her knowledge to them and evaluate their conformity to it.

5. Individual differences among people increase with age; therefore, adult education must make optimal provision for differences in style, time, place, and pace of learning.

Lindeman's ideas of adult learning had their beginning in 1926 and continued to show forth in the pages of the *Journal of Adult Education,* the quarterly publication of the American Association of Adult Education (Knowles, 1984). The beauty of concepts that are imbedded in truth is they stand the test of time.

How Do Adults Learn?

A. M. Tough's investigation was concerned not only with what and why adults learn, but how they learn and what help they obtain for learning. Tough found that adult learning is a very pervasive activity. His research revealed that almost everyone undertakes at least one or two major learning efforts a year and some individuals undertake as many as 15 or 20: It is common for a man or a woman to spend 700 hours a year at learning projects. About 70% of all learning projects are planned by the learner himself, who seeks help and subject matter from a variety of acquaintances, experts, and printed resources (Tough, 1979). Tough found that his subjects organized their learning efforts around "projects," a series of related episodes, that add up to at least seven hours. In each instance, more than half of the person's total motivation is to gain and retain certain knowledge and skill or to produce some other lasting change (Tough, 1967, 1979, 1982).

21

Positioned for the Exchange

The andragogical model has been successfully applied in North America, Europe, Africa, Brazil, and Australia with individuals from every socioeconomic level. It is comprehensive in its scope and content. It has been applied in situations dealing with scientific and technical content along with those of humanities and social sciences. Tough's seminal studies of self-directed learning (1967,1971) and subsequent studies by Penland (1977) and Peters (1974) stimulated numerous studies around the world. Tough (1979) cites twenty studies completed in the previous decade. These studies found that adults do engage in self-directed learning outside formal instructional programs, but adults assume a dependent role when they engage in structured educational activities. M. I. Cheren (1978) found that adults learn to take more control of their own learning and that there is a "transitional dynamic" that can be facilitated. There is now good reason to believe that self-directed learning is the natural mode when adults learn things on their own. Thus the andragogical model is a natural method of learning by adults.

R. D. Bowers (1977), in a study of 474 students at Boston University, found that adult students tend to respond more positively to andragogical methods regardless of age, marital status, estimated grade point average, graduate/undergraduate status, or class size. The application of andragogical principles in the university class tends to predict increased cognitive and affective learning as perceived by students. Bender and Darkenwald (1982) found that teachers do teach adults differently from children and adolescents. Specifically, when teaching adults, teachers appeared to emphasize responsive learner-centered behaviors with little emphasis toward controlling and structuring behaviors. Much of the PHAT STAR adult workshop entails responsive interaction. The concept of self-directed learning and life situations allows for the continued involvement of adults, they feel as if they are part of the development of the curricula they are learning from.

Workshops Hosted by the Church

Malcolm Knowles (1984) believes that Eugene Trester, director of the Biblical Andragogy Clinic in Mississauga, Ontario addresses how a community atmosphere strengthens adult education. Trester speaks of four special features of the clinic. They are as follows:

1. The challenge to religious educators of adult learners,
2. Focus on learning, not teaching,
3. Formation of learning communities,
4. Leadership training through facilitators' clinics.

He points out that contemporary Biblical scholarship alerts us to the fact that the Bible was formed in a community context. Adult learning theorists emphasize that adults learn best in a community atmosphere fostering cooperation, caring and mutual respect. Malcolm Knowles speaks of Eugene Trester's article entitled "The Biblical Andragogy Clinic" Trester suggest what he felt could alleviate a contemporary religious education problem: churches and synagogues relying on the development of small communities of adult learners. The concept that specialized in Biblical studies should be used to nurture and empower people in their day-to-day living. The integration of scientific advancements in religious knowledge into contemporary adult life is a prerequisite for vital adult faith and for balanced mental health. "Adults need to live their religious lives in the present age" (Knowles, 1984). PHAT STAR church sponsored workshops encourage individuals to search the scriptures for answers and empowerment when it comes to their relevant issues. The Apostle Peter refers to God's divine power granting us everything pertaining to life and godliness, through the true knowledge of Him who has called us by His own glory and excellence (2 Peter 1:3).

Positioned for the Exchange

Informed adult Christians are indispensable to the challenge of translating Christian values and attitudes into social, political, and economic institutions (Cooke, 1976). Simmons (1976, 1978) observed that, in the venture of religious growth, individual adults need the assistance of a sponsoring community. It appears that one of the keys to Christianity's future is community; but essential to modern-day communities are competent, well-trained adults who live out their context of faith and experience. A primary goal of PHAT STAR adult workshops hosted by churches or para-church organizations is for the youth worker to be refreshed, strengthened, resourced and encouraged. Biblical andragogy (an adult Biblical interdependent learning program) is used in formatting all workbooks and activities in these sessions. The workshop provides insights of modern Biblical scholarly research in a community-learning context of positive affirmation. It was designed to be an on-the-spot leadership-training program that allows adults an exciting opportunity of interdependent, scholarly, Biblical learning in a supportive environment. The PHAT STAR church sponsored workshop allows each youth worker to be informed about adolescents from a biopsychosocial, theological perspective.

Effective Adult Learning

Malcolm Knowles (1984) emphasizes that successful adult learning is based on four points. One, adult learners want to learn skills that apply to practical, real-life situations. Two, adult learners are self-directed. Three, adults learn better through active learning, such as role-playing or case scenarios, than they do through lecture-based instruction. Four, adults are aware of their own learning.

In their reviews of adult learning research, Zemke and Zemke (1981, 1995) summarized several key points. Trainees who are taught a new skill are better able to retain the skill if they are given the opportunity to use the skill immediately; otherwise knowledge of the skill will fade. Our most effective workshops are designed to compliment an ongoing youth program or event. This allows the youth worker to implement what they have learned while they continue to meet with youth. Adults prefer classes that

24

focus on a single subject with the application of the subject to relevant problems. Adult learners are most receptive to training when they are employed in a position. It is beneficial to the adult to learn and apply information, participate in training classes based on what they already know, not run contrary to it. Otherwise, integration of the new material is much slower. Trainers are also encouraged to involve their trainees in the planning stages of training, such as asking what it is that they need to know to perform their jobs. In the development of PHAT STAR workshops and curricula an interactive qualitative analysis assessment was used to understand the youth workers perception of their needs.

Denning and Verschelden (1993) used a focus group to assess the training needs of child welfare workers, involving trainees in the planning process. One of the results of this study suggested that participants felt that they were stimulated more and learned more from interactive training sessions. The interactive method allows individuals whose pregnant words and ideas to stir life and encouragement in the other participants. The subjects also reported that they learned more when the training class used a variety of modalities—visual, auditory and kinesthetic.

The PHAT STAR adult workshop was designed to meet the requested need of youth workers in local communities through intervention and implementation. Once the leaders are trained they are empowered to train others also. This will hopefully uphold the concept of lifelong learning.

～ Chapter 2

An Ecological Perspective of Adolescent Risk Taking

Whenever our team would plan a trip to a school to compete coach would take into consideration many factors before determining a departure time. If the trip was a two-hour journey, and field events started at 9:00 A.M. Saturday morning, coach's decision has now become complex. The athletes, public transportation, parents, finances, weather conditions and the amount of time sitting while traveling have now become a factor. For example, an athlete that usually took the bus to school would now have to ask their parent or guardian to make arrangements. Decision making becomes complex. What if this was a parent's day off and they had an opportunity to sleep in. It could be they had to work in the morning and had no way to get their child to the school. Coach would consider car pool situations or ask a supportive parent of the booster club to assist with arrangements. Finances became an issue if money was needed for food or lodging. Questions like: "Is there enough in the budget to cover this overnight trip?" or "should the money be used for the district or regional meet?" If the decision was to travel the day of the meet, time was needed for our food to digest, and proper time to warm up and stretch. Traveling in the bus for a few hours was also a consideration. Weather conditions were a factor. For example; on a cold rainy day we would need more time. Coach reminded us to always have ample warm up time. If we were rushed and did not warm up properly the probability of injury would increase. Rather than be at risk for injury, the coaching staff, and athletes had decisions to make which involved other people and environmental conditions.

Each of us had an individual responsibility to make decisions to avoid the risk of injury. We all had different reasons for what put us at risk. However, there were some basic guidelines the team adjusted to. Fundamentally, "have plenty of time to warm up."

Just as athletes have certain reasons for what puts them at risk, researchers have individual sets of definitions for "at-risk" differentiating one group from another based upon select criteria. Some use family characteristics such as a *single-headed household, low socioeconomic status*; others use *school performance or problem behaviors;* while a number of researchers look at *aggressiveness in preschool or shyness* as predictors of future problems. Adolescent specialist Joy Dryfoos defines high risk as "having the attributes of a young person with low probabilities of gaining an education, getting a job, effectively parenting, or being able to participate in the political process" (Dryfoos, 1997).

The term ecological considers the human organism within its social and environmental context. Some of the factors taken into consideration are economic status, cultural background, and the general social environment where adolescents interact directly (Brofenbrenner, 1979). These are called micro-systems, which include peers, family members, and social institutions such as schools and / or churches. The system of relations between these immediate settings is called meso-systems. For example, how does a 15-year-old female's relationship with her friends who are involved in deviant activity affect her relationship with her family members, her schoolwork or church youth group involvement? More distal, social environments such as community, mass media and social policies are called exo-systems. This setting does not directly involve the 15 year old but affects the setting in which she lives. The focus of PHAT STAR Education is to encourage and empower individuals in the micro-system of adolescents; parents, peers, professors and in some cases the parish (church affiliation) to better understand and communicate with each other. Empowering these individuals will improve linkage and transition with the adolescent in a positive manner. The macro-systems pertaining to culture, race, socio-economic systems and political contexts have been the focus of much research in conjunction with micro-systems. Through PHAT STAR Education there will be an opportunity to investigate the relationships that link and connect to one another while reaching the teen (the meso-system). In order to investigate the connections we must observe parts that make up the whole. The next section will describe what data reveals concerning peers, parents and other micro-systems.

Peer Influence

Peers play an increasingly important role in the socialization and development of teenagers. High school students in the United States and Europe spend twice as much time each week with peers as with parents or other adults even discounting time in class at school (Brown, Theobad, & Klute, in press; Larson and Verma, 1999). Virtually all adolescents spend most of each weekday with their peers while at school. The vast majority also see or talk to their friends in the afternoon, evening, and over the weekend. In contemporary America and Europe, however, age segregation is the norm, a fact of life that is clearly reflected in the tremendous amount of time that teenagers spend with their peers (Larson & Verma, 1999).

The separation of adolescents from adults has been fueled by the rise in the maternal employment. In European suburban neighborhoods mothers having to move from the home into the workplace furthered the trend toward the development of residential neighborhoods dominated by young people during weekday mornings and afternoons. Perhaps the most important factor is the rise of adolescent peer groups in recent years has been the rapid growth of the teenage population between 1955 and 1975, a trend that repeated itself during the 1990's. Research distinguishes between crowds and cliques amongst adolescents. Crowds are larger than more vaguely defined groups that are based on reputation (Brown, 1990). Contrary to the stereotyped homogeneous youth culture, research has indicated that the social world of adolescents is made up of many diverse subcultures (Mory, 1992, Brown et al., 1994).

PHAT STAR Education is committed to empowering adults concerned about today's youth with an understanding of how peers influence adolescent development, as well as being able to identify which peer group a teen is a part of.

Parents

Parents also have been viewed as important elements of the adolescent micro-system. The majority of adolescents feel close to their parents, respect their judgment, feel their parents love and care about them, and have a lot of respect for them as individuals (Steinberg, 2001). According to the YMCA telephone survey conducted for the White House Conference on Teenagers, one-fifth of American teenagers say that their top concern is that they don't have enough time with their parents; ironically, less than one-tenth of parents say that their top concern is that they don't have enough time with their kids (YMCA, 2000).

Research reveals that adolescents and their parents have similar beliefs about the importance of hard work, educational and occupational ambitions, and about the personal characteristics and attributes that they feel are important and desirable (Gecas & Seff, 1990). Socioeconomic background, for instance, has much stronger influence on individuals' values and attitudes than does age, and adolescents are more likely to share their parents' values than those of other teenagers who are from a different background. Wealthy adolescents growing up in affluent suburbs, for example, have educational and career plans that resemble their parents' plans for them, and their plans are very different from those of poor adolescents growing up in less prosperous areas (Gecas & Seff, 1990; Montemayor, 1983, 1984).

Even though topics of disagreement are similar across ethnic groups, conflict between adolescents and parents is generally less frequent in ethnic minority than non-minority, families (Barber, 1994; Kupersmidt, Burchinal, Leff, & Patterson, 1992). According to Judith Smetana and colleagues, when parents and adolescents disagree, it tends to be over mundane, day-to-day issues and not over major values or priorities. Different perspectives drawn into a conversation aids conflict. Parents typically see the issues as matters of right and wrong, and their children see them as personal choice (Smetana, 1988a, 1988b, 1989; Smetana & Asquith, 1994; Yau & Smetana, 1996).

Parenting Styles

According to psychologist Diana Baumrind (1978) and Maccoby & Martin (1983), there are four basic styles of parenting during adolescence: *authoritative parents,* who are warm but firm in setting standards for their child, but form expectations that are consistent with the child's developing needs and capabilities. *Authoritarian parents* place high value on obedience and conformity and tend to favor more absolute, forceful disciplinary measures. *Indulgent parents* are more accepting and benign and somewhat more passive in their disciplinary matters by placing relatively few demands on their children's behavior. This gives them a high degree of freedom to act as they choose. *Indifferent parents* try to do whatever is necessary to minimize the time and energy that they must devote to interacting with their child. It is important to note that authoritative parenting, which has been shown beneficial to adolescents from a variety of ethnic backgrounds, is composed of three main factors: warmth, structure, and autonomy support.

Children of authoritative (demanding and responsive) parents are less likely to use substances than children with authoritarian (demanding but unresponsive) or permissive parents. Adolescents with neglecting and rejecting parents are the most likely to engage in substance abuse (Baumrind, 1991). Several researchers have pointed out the distinction between authoritative and authoritarian parenting may not always make sense

31

when applied to parents from other cultures as well as religious backgrounds (Smetana & Gaines, 1999; Hetherington, & Reiss, 1999).

Adolescents from single parent families are more likely to initiate intercourse and are less likely to use contraception than their peers from intact families (Hayes, 1987; Mosher & McNally, 1991). They also are more likely to engage in various forms of substance use (Flewelling & Bauman, 1990). We must note there are single parent homes which have solid authoritative structure who's children are not involved in at-risk behavior patterns. It is apparent that the family structure has changed significantly in the United States. In 1955, a working father, a housewife mother, and two or more school-aged children described the typical family. At that time 60% of the households in the U.S. fit this description. In 1985, only 7% of the families fit that description. Significant increases in the divorce rate, the number of children born to unmarried females, and the percent of mothers in the work force has changed the nature of the typical family (Brindis et al., 1992). It is important to note however that not all authors agree that changes in family structure have had a major impact on adolescent risk taking, arguing that other things, such as political and cultural changes, are more critical (Dryfoos, 1997).

There has been contradictory and mixed results pertaining to adoption research. Several studies from early research concluded that adopted individuals have many more psychological problems than individuals raised by their biological parents, more recent research from larger and more representative samples question this conclusion. The age at which a child is adopted is what makes a difference. There is a higher incidence of problems seen in adolescents adopted relatively later in childhood rather than at infancy. In general, adopted individuals show slightly higher rates of delinquency and substance use and poorer school performance, but lower rates of withdrawal and interpersonal problems, and higher rates of prosocial behavior (Sharma, McGue, & Benson, 1998). Whether a child is adopted

32

or not, the amount of nurturing and the style of parenting is a primary factor in their psychosocial development.

Teachers and the School Environment

Many of us view school as the educational institution, however just as home is the first place where social interaction takes place, schools are potentially important tools of social interaction. The greatest number of young people can be most easily reached through schools. For years, the study of schools has been extremely important to the policymakers and social scientists interested in influencing adolescent development. This is an area that needs to become just as important to the parent as well as the parish. In the family and church (religious institution) there is also a strong sense of responsibility to train up and empower the next generation.

With every decade that adults felt a need for adolescents to change there was some type of school reform. For example, during the 1950's, when politicians felt that the United States had lost its scientific edge to the former Soviet Union, schools were challenged to see to it that the students took more science and math courses (Conant, 1959). When social scientists felt that adolescents were growing up unfamiliar with the world of work—as they did in the 1970's—schools were asked to provide opportunities for work-study programs and classes in career education (President's Science Advisory Committee, 1974). It was important for parents to be aware of what was being offered to their children. In some impoverished districts, courses were not being taught as they were in wealthy school districts. Community organizations and churches, once aware, could take an active role in the education process. In the 1990's as society struggled with a broad display of social problems affecting and involving youth in violence, AIDS and drug abuse, schools were looked to for assistance in implementing a wide variety of interventions (Dryfoos, 1993). Toward the end of the 1990's numerous inner-city schools were not producing graduates who could compete for high skill jobs, and in response to a public that was growing increasingly interested in alternatives to public education, schools were called upon to raise standards for all students (Ravitch, 2001). There is an opportunity for the church to get involved in empowering the young people and adults of their community. The facilities can be used for after school programs and adult education if necessary.

Secondary education (middle school, junior high, and high schools) has been the brunt of much criticism and scrutiny. Parents, teachers, educational administrators and researchers debate what schools should teach, how they should teach and how the schools should be organized. For example, should the school stick to instructing students in basics—reading, writing, and arithmetic—or should the students be offered a more diverse range of classes and services designed to prepare young people for adulthood socially, emotionally as well as intellectually? These questions have proven difficult to answer yet they are extremely important. Herein lies the rationale for empowering each people group within the micro-system.

A Biopsychosocial Model

Many causal factors of adolescent risk-taking behavior have been investigated and research reveals physical and psychological changes at puberty which impact adolescent risk taking. According to Urie Bronfenbrenner (1979), we cannot understand development without examining the settings, or the context, in which it occurs. Irwin and Millstein have designed a causal model of adolescent risk-taking behavior showing the tremendous impact that social support, or lack thereof, will have in the life of a teen. The model proposes that the timing of biological maturation directly influences four psychosocial factors: cognitive scope, self-perceptions, perceptions of the social environment and personal values. These four are hypothesized to predict adolescent risk-taking behavior through the mediating effects of risk perception and peer group characteristics. Irwin and Millstein (1986) define risk-taking as "volitional behaviors in which the mechanism for onset and maintenance form an interaction of

34

maturational forces of the adolescent and the environment. These risk-taking behaviors may produce uncertain consequences and negating health outcomes" (p. 82S). The role of the environment is an important predictor in the onset of risk behavior. The protective role of supportive environments during adolescence must be acknowledged and may be critical in developing prevention and intervention programs. Research indicates that family and peer factors are crucial, with parental behavior and style being important correlates of onset (Irwin, 1987).

Professional literature also shows that there are disposition-based theories of risk-taking which focus on individual differences that may be associated with a tendency to engage in risky behaviors. With many of these theories, risk taking is viewed as anomalous and pathological, reflecting a form of maladaptive functioning due to some problem within the individual. Researchers have hypothesized deficits such as poor self-esteem (Kaplan, 1980; Kaplan, Johnson & Bailey, 1987), depression, inadequate social skills (Botvin, 1986), impulsivity (McCord, 1990) or a general tendency toward unconventional activity and deviance (Donovan & R. Jessor, 1985; Osgood, Johnston, O' Malley & Bachman, 1988).

There is some evidence that many of the causal factors may be associated with engaging in risky behaviors under certain conditions. However, results are not always conclusive and are often contradictory. Despite the common acceptance of poor self-esteem as a causal factor and its introduction into many "affective" intervention programs (Dryfoos, 1990), current research suggests that self-esteem does not always translate into health-enhancing or prosocial behaviors. It has been suggested that risk-taking can raise self-esteem (Kaplan, 1980; Kaplan et al., 1987; McCord, 1990).

Theories of sensation-seeking (Zuckerman & Eysenck, 1978; Zuckerman, 1979) posit that people differ in terms of their underlying need for stimulation and that thrill-seeking underlies much of risk-taking behavior. The individuals who are considered thrill-seekers are willing to take risks if it will enhance stimulation and arousal. Sensation-seeking has been associated with

35

substance abuse and dangerous motor vehicle use in adolescents (Zuckerman, Ball & Black, 1990).

Jessor and Jessor have argued that the relatively greater influence of peers, as compared to parents, is associated with a greater tendency toward risk-taking behaviors (Jessor & Jessor, 1977). Some research supports the claim of relative dominance of peer influence over parental influence to predictive marijuana use, problem drinking and early sexual intercourse (Jessor & Jessor, Costa, Donovan, 1983).

Chapter 3

The Macro-System: Socio-Economic Status and the Adolescent

The relay team at our high school was comprised of young people from different economic backgrounds. Our coach never addressed our financial or neighborhood backgrounds during workouts. The focus was always what each of us had potential to contribute for a maximum team effort. This chapter will reveal data that supports how poverty can affect young people, but also depicts how the lives and health of adolescents are affected by the quality of their environment. We will also note the way young people live their lives can influence their environment.

The persistence of poverty is seen more with children of color, who tend to live in isolated, poor, urban neighborhoods where institutional supports for families and children are relatively scarce, and threats to positive growth and development are thought to be more abundant than with Euro-Americans (Garbarino, 1992). The economic contrast between the richest and poorest families in the United States appears to have increased in the last couple of decades. The rich got richer, and the poor got poorer. According to the 1999 U.S Census Bureau, March Current Population Survey, the percentage of children living in families experiencing extreme poverty was 7% in 1980.

This percentage rose to 10% in 1993 and has since decreased to 6% in 1999. Concurrently, three times as many children live in families with very high income in 1999 compared with 1980 (12% and 4%, respectively).

Generally, researchers hypothesize that living in a community, which has a high proportion of poor families, affects adolescents for the worse, regardless of their own family's situation. For instance, even if an adolescent lives in an economically stable, supportive household, he or she may be adversely affected by growing up in a community that has a high unemployment rate (because there are fewer employed role models with whom to identify), few resources such as libraries and museums and a high crime rate (National Research Council, 1993). Poverty no longer can be treated as a unidimensional incident nor is it assumed to be identical to low socioeconomic status. Researchers are increasingly sensitive to the fact that the impact of poverty can vary with race, gender, and ethnicity. The use of an ecological approach to human development with multiple levels of analysis is now taken seriously; many studies go beyond the individual child and parent to such contextual influences as school, neighborhood, and community.

Growing up in poverty may dramatically impair a youngster's ability to move easily between adolescence and adulthood. Poverty is associated with failure in school, unemployment, and out-of-wedlock pregnancy, all of which contribute to transitional difficulties (Edelman & Ladner, 1991; National Research Council, 1993). Growing up amid poverty early in life has a strong effect on individuals' cognitive ability; experiencing poverty during adolescence has an especially negative effect on young people's school achievement (Guo, 1998). In another chapter of the book we will look at reasons why the statistics could be revealing this data, and what communities can do to make a difference.

The outcome of studies has expanded beyond cognitive and intellectual development, to encompass socioemotional functioning. Poverty variables are found to have statistically significant effects on the quality of the home environment, after controlling for the effects of other variables in the models. Statistically significant interactions among poverty variables are identified. A major finding is that improvements in family income have the strongest effects on the quality of the home environment for children who were born poor or lived much of their lives in poverty (Phillips, 1991). In part two of the book I discuss the holistic STAR model, it is designed to encourage the church and other organizations to recognize their role to meet the need of individuals living in poverty. The mind of the people must be transformed while their hearts are encouraged. The physical conditions are difficult for many individuals. Therefore there is a need for economic empowerment along with other coping skills.

Economic stress in mothers was associated with higher levels of perceived financial strain, which in turn predicted adolescents' perceptions of economic hardship. Adolescents who perceived their families as experiencing more severe economic hardship reported higher anxiety, more cognitive distress, and lower self-esteem (McLoyd, Jayratne, Ceballo & Borquez, 1994). There is growing evidence that coming of age amid concentrated poverty has negative effects on adolescent behavior and mental health, as well as on the transition to adulthood. These effects are above and beyond those attributable to growing up in impoverished communities. They are more likely than their peers from equally poor households, but better neighborhoods, to bear children as teenagers and to achieve less in, or even drop out of high school (Leventhal & Brooks-Gunn, 2000). The absence of affluent neighborhoods, rather than the presence of poor neighborhoods, places an adolescent in impoverished communities at greatest academic risk (Duncan, 1994; Ensminger et al., 1996). To the extent that poverty increases behavior problems, adolescents living in poor neighborhoods come into contact with deviant peers all the more often. Adolescents who associate in these crowds are more likely to participate in criminal delinquent activity in the peer group (Simmons, Johnson, Beaman, Conger, & Whitbeck, 1996). It is important to note not all poor neighborhoods have high rates of juvenile crime. One study indicates that inner city adolescents growing up in moderately poor neighborhoods are more at risk for antisocial behavior than those growing up in extremely poor neighborhoods (Seidman et al., 1998). One must note that it is exposure to violence, rather than living in a poor neighborhood, that increases adolescents' risk for aggression (Paschall & Hubbard, 1998).

Irwin and Millstein and other researchers believe that a child's parentage and environment play a significant role in how a young person's personality and attitude about wellness are developed. The neighborhood of the youth has quite an impact on what health behaviors are encouraged (Irwin & Millstein, 1986; Irwin, 1987). The lives and health of adolescents are affected by the quality of their environment, and the way they live their lives influences the environment. The quality of a home in which a child is raised, (even in the midst of poverty) can impact the outcome of their education and behavior patterns as they transition to adulthood. The attitudes about sexuality, drug, alcohol and tobacco abuse and violence among adolescents influences their environment; and some of these environmental factors in the cities of America affect the decision making of the residential youth as well. Research demonstrates the necessity of intervention programs that honestly address issues in an age—and culturally—appropriate manner. Educators must work with their communities to best meet the needs of today's adolescent. The effort to encourage collaboration between community organizations, the home and school is a priority for PHAT STAR education. This chapter opened with the example of my high school coach who chose not to address our individual financial or neighborhood backgrounds during workouts, but focused on the potential each of us had to contribute to the maximum team effort.

~~~ Chapter 4

Cultural Diversity and Multicultural Education

When school let out, and it was time for us to report to practice, we would gather in the locker room. Our conversation was either about the last class of the day, or what kind of workout coach was going to put us through. Each of us knew what our specific duties were on the team. Our workouts would differ depending on the event we competed in. When it was time to practice relay exchanges, our training was similar. Our different skills would be joined together for the advancement of the team. PHAT STAR community workshops allow individuals from diverse cultures and backgrounds to voluntarily come together sharing their gifts, ideas and talents. Through facilitated training and forums the individuals are equipped, empowered and enabled to invest in the next generation. When it comes to the four by one hundred relay, no one individual is the hero of the team. And in a local community, concerned adults should represent every people group living therein. Sharing concerns of the youth and learning ways to mediate difficulties while celebrating their achievements, will prove beneficial for generations to come.

Positioned for the Exchange

Multicultural collaborative dialogue and training allow individuals, especially educators, to systematically analyze their instructional behaviors and implement new ones. The concept of the workshop is to encourage the youth worker to view all young people from a holistic culturally relevant perspective.

Cultural influences need to be counteracted by developing skills in critical consciousness and culturally appropriate pedagogy for use with diverse young people. Several chapters in the *Handbook of Research on Multicultural Education* (Banks & Banks, 1995), explain what this means specifically for Native Americans, African Americans, and Mexican Americans. Banks' book does discuss the importance of teaching about the cultural heritages and contributions of ethnic groups of concern. It appears throughout the research that culturally appropriate or responsive pedagogy empowers individuals intellectually, socially, emotionally, and politically by using cultural referents to impart knowledge, skills, and attitudes (Ladson-Billings, 1992). According to Banks (1997), teacher re-education or training of adult leaders in the area of multicultural education has four primary emphases. The first being *self-knowledge*. He believes that teachers, counselors, and administrators need to become conscious of their own cultural values and beliefs, and how these affect their attitudes and expectations toward different ethnic groups. It is important to note how these behaviors are habitually exhibited in their interaction among the youth. This principle is vital for all youth workers who are working in diverse communities. It is essential to understand the effects our attitudes and expectations have on young people, relative to their self-concepts, academic abilities, educational opportunities, and achievement outcomes. Having what Spindler and Spindler (1993) call a cultural consciousness is imperative in order to anticipate potential conflicts, misunderstandings, and blind spots in the perception and interpretation of behavior. For many youth workers this could be the first step in changing insensitive, biased behaviors, attitudes and assumptions that are detrimental to youth whose cultural backgrounds are different from their own. It also enhances co-laboring relationships with those in diverse communities. The emphasis must be that social reform begins with the individual. We each must see the value of learning one from another as we endeavor to meet the needs of a diverse youth community. The value of PHAT STAR training is that we are not merely telling youth workers about how cultural assumptions can lead to low expectations and negative consequences for young people of color, but the workshop setting allows them opportunities to process and work out practically how they behave toward individuals of a different culture.

The second emphasis given by James Banks in teacher reeducation *understands the differences in cultural values and behavioral codes between European middle-class Americans and students of color.* The process of reeducation begins with acquiring knowledge about the adolescent's cultural background, life experiences, and interaction styles to replace racial myths and stereotypes that could be present. Studies reveal that knowledge of cultural diversity is an essential foundation for equality and excellence in both the process and outcomes of education. The findings consistently indicate that where there is "cultural connectedness" in the educational process, academic achievement of students of color improves (Gay, 1994). The beauty of church hosted workshops is that there is a challenge and emphasis upon our similarities. These are what I could call the "people things." We must be willing to address the differences while focusing on the similarities of being God's child. Research supports academic achievement fosters resiliency to the consequences of negative risk-taking behavior (Dryfoos, 1997; Werner & Smith, 1982). The anticipated desire is for the youth worker to make the cultural connection to ultimately decrease the number of youth who experience school failure.

The third reeducation focus of Banks addressed in a PHAT STAR workshop is *the development of technical instructional skills that are appropriate for use with a multicultural student population.* This knowledge is to be combined with learning how to diversify teaching strategies culturally and to create a more supportive environment for learning and demonstrating achievement, to reduce stress, tension, and conflict that may be present in the school classroom. Youth leaders are introduced to holistic, preventive education, learning materials that are meaningful, involving, enabling and empowering for a diverse population youth.

The fourth emphasis of Banks for the retraining of teachers, counselors, and school administrators for educational equality is *public relations skill development*. A strong emphasis of PHAT STAR community workshops is improvement of parent communication among youth workers serving in after-school programs, churches, and school classroom teachers. In many school districts there is a gap between the professionals and the parent—youth today are not under any adult's direct tutelage "twenty-four-seven." There is a benefit to collaborative efforts in a local community. Some of us have background information, but limited experience from a cultural theological perspective. This methodology is designed to expose those working with youth to several things: self-directed learning, effective communication with youth, a self-diagnosis of the level of confidence of the youth worker and the identification of relevant resources and lesson planning. It is important to note that for many years we as youth workers have acted independently calling our own shots. But now we have an opportunity to enter in to a larger more integrated environment.

Postmodern Society and Multicultural Education

"One more time ladies!" These were familiar words from the infield of the stadium as we worked on relay exchanges. There were numerous reasons for a "bad" handoff: the incoming runner fails to communicate or slows down before reaching the fly zone; the outgoing runner takes off too soon, or does not position their hand properly. When the baton was not properly exchanged, frustration would build. It took multiple drills for a proper handoff. There are times when the communication from scholars, to schools and parents, is similar to a bad relay exchange. Sometimes the message of the child's need is not properly communicated.

Cultural Diversity and Multicultural Education

Research of numerous family programs verifies that parents of high-risk youth will come to schools and community centers if what they are offered is useful and non-threatening. Community schools have proven that virtually all the parents will come to an ethnic or cultural celebration. Many parents participate in educational or life skills courses; some examples are English as a second language, computers, job preparation, and aerobics. Even though these courses are successful, many of the same parents are ignorant to their child's academic placement. Communication always has room for improvement. With a better understanding of our postmodern culture and multicultural education, we can better discern if our children are receiving what will empower them for the future.

While there are many concepts of postmodernism and much confusion about it's meaning, there are some common characteristics. The Center for a Post-Modern World believes postmodernism regards the world as an organism rather than a machine, the earth as a home rather than as isolated and independent. David Ray Griffin and colleagues believe postmodernism refers to a diffuse sentiment rather than to any set of common doctrines—the sentiment that humanity can and must go beyond the modern (Griffin et al. 1993). There appears a need for a paradigmatic shift in thinking that must accompany postmodern consciousness. The postmodern worldview allows educators to envision a way out of the turmoil of contemporary schooling that is often characterized by violence, depersonalized evaluation, political conflict, economic crisis, decaying infrastructure, emotional fatigue, demoralization of personnel and hopelessness.

It is beneficial for curriculum to have much of its theoretical base in postmodernism. It is viewed as a cyclical process where the past and future inform and enrich the present rather than a linear structure where events can be isolated, analyzed and objectified. For example, when working with African American adolescents, having an understanding of the cultural historical struggles and strengths may prove to be very valuable in how you reach and teach your students. There is a growing recognition that the educational community cannot address the hopelessness, poverty, injustice, violence and ecological devastation that plague the cities of America and contribute to the decay of the social milieu of schools by simply reacting to the symptoms. Traditional curriculum development models focus on external, tangible, measurable items and tend to ignore the ethical, ecological, sociological and economic crisis that threatens society. PHAT STAR speaks to these issues while endeavoring to equip the youth worker with relevant concepts and tools. For example, just because an individual can repeat information does not mean they have learned or understand the concept or the context from which their answer develops.

Curriculum scholar David Purpel contends that the moral and spiritual crisis in society must be at the forefront of curriculum studies and postmodern schooling must attend these important issues (Purpel, 1989). Harvey Cox (1984), shares the view that postmodern education is linked to religion in the secular society. His proposal flows out of the tradition of "problem-posing" pedagogy established in Latin America by the Brazilian educator Paulo Freire (1970), who viewed the problems of education as inseparable from political, social, and economic problems. Peasants were encouraged to examine critically their life situations and take initiative to transform social structures that denied them meaningful civic participation. Freire's (1971) manuscript "Conscientizing as a Way of Liberating" is considered one of the important philosophical foundations of liberation theology. Liberation theology has utilized Freire's pedagogy to establish *communautes de base* (base communities) that unite religious reflection with social action, as a form of praxis that can inspire lasting change in the Latin American community. In 1984, Harvey Cox and colleagues Hans Kung, and theologian Mark Taylor proposed a "postmodern theology" (Cox, 1984).

Modern educational reforms continue to be committed to scientific and technical methodologies with an emphasis on measurable outcomes. However, postmodern educators recognize that the crises that has plagued schools in the past will not be resolved by the exclusive use of any of the modern reform proposals thrust upon education in the past century, often by those committed to the continuation of modernity in government, business, industry, and military (Kliebard, 1986; Shea et al., 1989; Pinar, 1988). The contributions of spirituality, theology and religion are now beginning to be incorporated into new postmodern revisions.

The incorporation of spirituality, theology, and religious education into postmodern visions of schooling is not universally and uncritically accepted. The suppression of theology, spirituality and religious education in modern public and private schools has been evidenced in numerous ways—the long history of tolerance of racism and sexism (Ruether, 1983; Pinar, 1988), irresolvable conflicts over moral issues in modern technological society, and the tradition of separation of church and state (Cox, 1984; Whitson, 1991). The theological premise of all mankind, is that we are created equal, but designed different for a different purpose. It does not appear as though postmodern scholars have discovered a way out of the modern dilemma of religion and schooling and thus have often excluded spirituality and theology from their curriculum proposals. While time passes on, there appears to be an opportunity for the church to take an active role with its young people again. Educational systems continue to debate issues of separation of church and state and the concepts of morality in teaching. The time is right for prevention and intervention programs to collaborate with the church.

Research shows some notable exceptions to this trend. David Ray Griffin (1988a) has called for public life to reflect religious values in his postmodern proposals. David Purpel (1989) has challenged teachers to become prophets who orient the educational process toward a vision of ultimate meaning and "infuse education with the sacred" (p. 105). John I. Goodlad has proposed that the educational community include a vision of morality and values in teacher education programs. Curricular specialist David G. Smith (1988) believes that education must not simply tell us what we are, but most significantly, what we hope to become. Smith writes, "attention to the eidetic quality of our life together is an attempt to bring into the center of our research conversation everything that we are, as a way of reconciling in the present moment our ends with our beginnings" (p. 435). For years there has been dialogue concerning behavior change and what causes an individual to act the way they do. Is it nature and genetics, or nurture and environment? As youth educators and mentors have an opportunity to teach the concept of understanding the origin of mankind. Philip Phenix (1975) has pointed out the significance for schooling of the "lure of transcendence toward wholeness" (p.333). William Doll (1993) suggests that the postmodern curriculum is imbued with an astral character that leads to personal and spiritual transformation (Doll, 1993). The Apostle Paul encouraged the individuals living in Rome in a similar fashion. He told them—God helping you take your everyday, ordinary life and place it before God as an offering. Embrace what God has done for you. Instead become so well adjusted to the culture of the day that you fit into it without thinking. Instead fix your attention on God. You'll be changed from the inside out.

Modern science has come full circle since the eighteenth century rejection of religion as a hindrance to the development of modern scientific progress by Pierre Simon de Laplace and others, to realization that religious questions are at the very heart of science (Griffin, 1988a, 1988b). While religion has traditionally been associated with denominational practices and beliefs, theology is sometimes considered a more systematic and rational study of faith and the holy as related to patterns of meaning that prevail in a historical period or culture (Cox, 1984). Spirituality is associated with the realm of personal faith and supernatural revelation. Where the public school is not ready for this, the church has a wonderful opportunity to integrate spirituality into the overall development of young people.

The understanding of curriculum that is proposed in postmodernism is not restricted to the modern program of studies in the schools of the twentieth century as codified in textbooks, guides, scopes and sequences, and behavioral lesson plans. Rather, the verb form of curriculum, *currere,* which refers to running of the race rather than the racecourse itself, is primary. *Currere* emphasizes the individual's own capacity to reconceptualize his or her autobiography, recognize connections with other people, recover and reconstitute the past, imagine and create possibilities for the future, and come to a greater personal and communal awareness. According to Donald Oliver and Kathleen Gershman, this awareness grounds an individual's knowledge in being, not in methods or techniques. From this postmodern perspective, the curriculum as *currere* is an interpretation of lived experiences rather than a static course of studies to be completed (Oliver & Gershman, 1989). For example when young people have a sense of purpose and destiny it will give them the opportunity to view life's experiences as a part of shaping their destiny. Where there is no vision or dream young people will have no boundaries or restraints.

Reorganizing responsibility and authority does not address the theological issue of how to confront cultural malaise, despair, and fear in modern American society. Patrick Slattery believes that a reconceptualization of religious education that includes a synthesis of community models of education is emerging. For public schools this would reflect the empowerment models found in programs like the Dade County Florida Public Schools (Dreyfuss et al., 1992) or the Windham Southeast District in Vermont (James et al., 1992). The curriculum as a theological text provides expanded opportunities for students and teachers to explore alternative solutions to the ecological, health and economic problems of the world today. The traditional behavioral-technical curriculum of the public school system, which many private school boards and administrators are so apt to imitate, is seen as outmoded and inappropriate for all school systems.

Postmodern schools flow out of school architecture, school schedules, teacher attitudes, and classroom environments that encourage flexibility, critical literacy, ethics, autobiography, ecumenism, global interdependence, ecological sustainability, narrative inquiry and other postmodern values. Hopefully through workshop training, teacher's attitudes are stimulated to become facilitators of learning encouraging young people to reason toward conclusions. When this takes place they are becoming facilitators rather than information givers. Reflective dialogue with grandparents, younger students, multicultural professionals, community activists, politicians, and religious leaders should be regular occurrences. Active community involvement in environmental projects, health and social services, and ethnic preservation will become a priority (Slattery, 1992b). In *Exiles from Eden: Religion and the Academic Vocation in America,* Mark R. Schewehn (1945) writes that achieving community at the end of modernity and the beginning of postmodernity means connecting to virtues and experiences that have traditionally been thought to be spiritual. Yvonna Lincoln (1994) in a review of Schewehn's book points out that there are spiritual values equally essential to "the process of genuine learning (and therefore meaningful teaching). Those virtues—faith, humility (piety), charity, self-denial, and friendship—tend to be both social virtues and those that sustain genuine communities" (p. 36). Schwehn argues that education must be attentive to these virtues or all attempts at internal reformation will prove ultimately useless. The virtues that Schwehn speaks of that are essential to the process of genuine learning are similar to a letter written to a group of Corinthians. They were told to trust steadily in God, hope unswervingly, love extravagantly. And the best of the three is love.

Cultural Awareness and the Shaping of Perceptions and Expectations

How a person thinks, feels and what they will to do has a lot to do with the shaping of their perceptions. In a model designed to reach and teach people of a certain community, there must be a cultural awareness of how behaviors, values and ideas are shaped. Curriculum development and program design in this postmodern era should give place to the uniqueness of each individual person, text, event, culture, and educative moment, but all within the context of an interdependent cosmological view. There was a growing body of curriculum research which emerged from scholars sensitive to issues related to race and culture, Peter McLaren and Michael Dantley (1990), Keith Osajima (1992),

Barry Troyna and Richard Hatcher (1992), and Lois Weis (1983, 1988). Race and gender will continue to be central issues to understand curriculum development. It is important to note the difference between human and civil rights. When referring to human rights all mankind is involved and the focus of injustice should be looked at in light of male and female created in the image of God. Fordham and Ogbu (1986) indicate that personal and cultural knowledge is problematic when it conflicts with scientific ways of validating knowledge, or when it is in opposition to the culture of the program or challenges the tenets and assumptions of how things have always been done. The development and testing of a theory is highly dependent on valid and reliable measurement of concepts. If theory is to be tested across cultures and socioeconomic strata, the relevant variables must have comparable meaning across the groups, in other words they must have *cultural equivalence* (Berry, 1969). As members of basic institutions of society—families, schools, churches, youth organizations, health care agencies, media, higher education, the scientific community, and government we have an opportunity to collaborate and meet the developmental needs of youth.

Part Two

United to Rebuild and Restore

~~~~ Chapter 5

The Call to Collaboration

The Team Uniform

*"Teamwork is the joint action by a group of people in which individual
interests are subordinated to group unity and efficiency"* ~ Webster

One of the most exciting days of the season as a high school
athlete was when our head coach gave the speech about
team pride and unity before handing out the uniforms. Coach
would distribute the articles of clothing to each athlete and re-
mind us of whom we were representing while in uniform. When
we would march into a stadium and warm up in a synchronized
manner, I would have an adrenaline rush as I sensed the unlimited potential of team unity. I later read a passage that described
my feeling: "Here they're one people, and they all have one language, and this is what they've begun to do. And now nothing
that they'll scheme to do will be precluded from them" (Genesis
11:5,6).

In the book of beginnings the Torah states: and YHWH (Yah-
way) went down to see the city and the tower that the children
of humankind had built. And YHWH said, "Here they're one

people, and they all have one language, and this is what they've begun to do. And now nothing that they'll scheme to do will be precluded from them." This was a powerful statement! In other words because the people were communicating with a like-mind, they had unlimited possibilities.

To work together effectively, we must be willing to relinquish our selfish ambitions for the betterment of the team. A relay team's success is formed, as each member strives to be of one mind united in spirit and intent on the purpose to run with excellence! In the recent tragedy that occurred September 11, 2001 America's response to terrorism was a united front against that which would crush our spirits. There were American flags, prayer meetings, continual words of encouragement and consolation from every culture and ethnic background, because we all had a common ground, the soil of America. Today, parents, youth workers, educators, program directors and role models must choose to lay aside our individualized programs and collaborate our ideas to best reach and teach this generation. Imagine the unlimited potential of a unified front waging war against ideologies, and societal pressures leading to the morbidity and mortality of today's youth. It will take a consistent collaborative effort for this kind of teamwork.

The Webster's definition spoke of teamwork as a joint action by a group of people. A joint is where two bones connect and are held together by ligaments. This tough fibrous tissue assures that the bones stay in place whenever pressure is applied to the joint. Communities today are more diverse than ever. The ligament that will hold such a diverse group of people together is the desire to impact the generation coming behind us, and the one yet to be born. The challenge of community collaboration is to work together in difficult times. Pressure prevails in the absence of unity. There is true collaboration when diversity and autonomy is present among individuals walking in unity. For example, some parents are educated bearing degrees from the finest universities and others are educated from life's experiences of serving people in the community for decades. Parents, ivory tower scholars, Sunday school teachers, medical doctors and classroom educators all have a part to play on the team!

On occasion when competing athletically, my focus would be altered because of friction with a teammate. However, something would happen the moment I stepped into my uniform. Thoughts would fill my mind of the most difficult practices we labored through. There would be a sober hush in the locker room as we got dressed. The tension lifted the minute we were on the track. The uniforms reminded us of our team connection. We were held together by the common interest, to run with excellence! If one of us participated in a field event, we would inform the proper official, and report for the relay, returning to our individual event after the relay had been run. As a team we would jog and work on exchanges, stretch together and report to the meet clerk. Each relay team would be lined up on the field and the clerk would make certain every team member's uniform looked alike. If one uniform did not match, the individual would have to make an adjustment or the team would be disqualified. When given the O.K. we were placed on the track in our assigned positions prepared to run our race with excellence.

In our endeavor to impact the next generation we must see ourselves as a team! There are times of individual sacrifice for the sake of reaching the youth of your community. The challenge is to encourage, console and strengthen one another in the midst of what may appear to be unfruitful. The nation is in need of a unified front, maintaining compassion, intent on the purpose of nurturing and developing the next generation. With humility of mind are we willing to esteem one another as more important than ourselves especially in areas where we lack skills?

Common unity should be encouraged between parents, school educators, churches, youth organizations, health care agencies, local merchants, and policy makers in hopes to meet the developmental needs of youth entrusted to their care. Are we committed, focused and willing to sacrifice personal preference for the good of the team? Our roles may differ, but the ultimate goal is the same. The Apostle Paul scribed similar thoughts to the church in Corinth when he said:

> For by one Spirit we were all baptized into one body—whether Jews or Greeks, whether slaves or free—and have all been made to drink into one Spirit. For in fact the body is not one member but many. If the foot should say, "Because I am not a hand, I am not of the body," is it therefore not of the body? And if the ear should say, "Because I am not an eye, I am not of the body," is it therefore not of the body? If the whole body were an eye, where would be the hearing? If the whole were hearing, where would be the smelling? But now God has set the members, each one of them, in the body just as He pleased. And if they were all one member, where would the body be? But now indeed there are many members, yet one body. And the eye cannot say to the hand, "I have no need of you"; nor again the head to the feet, "I have no need of you." No, much rather, those members of the body which seem to be weaker are necessary. And those members of the body, which we think to be less honorable, on these we, bestow greater honor; and our unpresentable parts have greater modesty, but our presentable parts have no need. But God composed the body, having given greater honor to that part which lacks it, that there should be no schism in the body, but that the members should have the same care for one another. And if one member suffers, all the members suffer with it; or if one member is honored, all the members rejoice with it." (1 Corinthians 12:13–27 NKJV)

This previous passage scribed to the Corinthians affirms the PHAT STAR collaborative philosophy: *Different individuals working together with equality of authority within their individual purpose of the cooperative effort.* In other words we all have a mentoring role at some time in the life of a young person.

Numerous biological, social and cultural factors affect the well being of youth in a community. The efficiency of serving them would depend on the ability of the community to organize and work together. Wallerstein and Sanchez-Merki's (1994) work with the Adolescent Social Action Program identified three stages an individual would pass from apathy to a social responsibility to act. In many communities it appears that individuals are apathetic, when in reality may not be aware of a problem, or how they can be involved to bring about any effective change. The first stage involves *individuals beginning to care about the problem, each other, and their ability to act in the world.* This must be preceded with information of the current conditions of youth in the nation, their local community or in their daily life (a child, or a student in their class). This stage is accomplished through dialogue and self-disclosure in small groups and through the use of questioning. The next stage is known as *individual responsibility to act.* It comes forth as individuals' self-efficacy to talk and help others increases. The improved self-efficacy is a result of participating in the caring dialogue with other community members who have similar experiences with youth in their life. The final stage, *social responsibility to act,* involves critical thinking about the social forces that underlie the problem, (this could be anything from the media, family issues, generational patterns, styles of discipline etc. . . .) and a commitment to engage in self and community change. As this three-stage process takes place it could result in individual and community empowerment.

In order to build community and meet the needs of today's youth there is a need for increased community competence, leadership development, and as Paulo Friere states a critical consciousness or awareness. PHAT STAR EDUCATION is committed to working with grass root organizations (made up of families in the community) and connecting them with professional public service organizations, lay clergy and health workers. Empowerment has taken place when individuals, communities and organizations change their social, and at times their political, environment. This comes about through a gained sense of efficacy, improved equity, and enhanced quality of life (Minkler & Wallerstein, 1997b).

Our relay team would spend hours working on technique. This meant showing up at practice, and sometimes we would sacrifice time spent on individual event training to work on perfecting our baton exchanges. Making transitions from home to school, church to home, medical clinic to home takes work! We must be willing to work together to make a positive impact! This work begins on the individual level—each of us asking ourselves, "What is my part in this collaborative effort?"

～ Chapter 6

Times, Trends and Teens

The Track Meet Conditions—What Are We Up Against?

In the preface of the book we discussed the relay race, and what makes for a smooth transition. There are always prerequisites to the competition. The coach of the team would have to consider the weather conditions and the design of the track prior to positioning his athletes in the relay. The weather conditions in this chapter refer to the current conditions of society and adolescents.

What Are the Conditions of the Playing Field?

Recent societal trends reveal strong effects on adolescent development. The most evident trends are the changing family, the shifting nature of work, the gap between early reproductive capacity and adult roles, and the influence of the media. As a nation into the early years of a new century, it appears that the progression of change will continue to accelerate. Innovative ways of adapting to new societal conditions must be created to ensure that diverse populations of youth in America have their basic needs met. There appears to be an absence of quality effective leadership in political, civic, economic, social and spiritual arenas throughout our communities in America. We must be cognizant that no individual is perfect. When a runner on our team was ineligible or injured, our coach would exhort us to fill in the gap. This meant each of us would have to sacrifice a little more time to adjust to the team member that stepped in. Our task in this collaborative effort is, when one team member is injured or ineligible, we who are in the community may have to fill in the gap and encourage others around us to pull together sacrificing where needed to invest quality and efficient help to the youth we serve. Too often, we exert a lot of energy complaining rather than collaborating.

Demographics

In 2000, there were 70.4 million children under the age of eighteen living in the United States, 0.2 million more than in 1999. This number is projected to increase to 77.2 million in 2020 the largest absolute number of youth in the nation's history. Children are projected to remain a stable percentage of the total population, comprising 24% of the population (U.S. Bureau of Census, 2000). Racial and ethnic diversity has grown dramatically in the United States in the last three decades. The increased diversity first manifests itself among children, and later in the older population. In 2000, 64% of United States children were white, non-Hispanic; 16% were Hispanic; 15% were black, non-Hispanic; 4% were Asian /Pacific Islander; and 1% were American Indian/ Alaska Native. The percentage of children who are white, non-Hispanic has decreased from 74% in 1980 to 64% in 2000. The percentages of black, non-Hispanic and American Indian/Alaska Native children have been fairly stable during the period from 1980 to 2000. The number of Hispanic children has increased faster than that of any other racial and ethnic group, growing from 9% of the child population in 1980 to 16% in 2000. By 2020, it is projected that more than 1 in 5 children in the United States will be of Hispanic origin.

Teen Pregnancy

Giving birth to a child during adolescence is often associated with long-term difficulties for the mother, her child, and society. Compared to babies born to older mothers, babies born to adolescents under the age of 18, particularly young adolescent mothers, are at higher risk of low birth weight and infant mortality. They (the children) are more likely to grow up in homes that offer lower levels of emotional support and cognitive stimulation, and they are less likely to earn high school diplomas. These consequences are often attributable to poverty and the other adverse socioeconomic circumstances that frequently accompany childbearing. It is imperative that young women of this nation be taught the facts. They must understand that with menarche (the ability to reproduce) comes responsibility. PHAT STAR curriculum focuses on understanding the purpose of our human design. For example if young people are taught the organs of the human reproductive system with an opportunity to process how, when and why each organ functions. I believe the art of reasoning through to understanding will enable them to stand under pressures that come their way.

In 1999, the adolescent birth rate was 44 per 1,000 unmarried women ages 15 to 44. Between 1980 and 1994, the birth rate for unmarried women ages 15 to 44 increased from 29 to 47 per 1,000. The rate has since stabilized; between 1994 and 1997-99 the rate fell slightly to 44 per 1,000. During 1980-94, birth rates increased sharply for unmarried women in all age groups. The birth rate for unmarried women ages 15 to 17 increased from 21 to 32 per 1,000, and the rate for unmarried women ages 18 to 19 rose from 39 to 70 per 1,000. In 1999, 33% of all births were to unmarried women.

The Changing Family

In 2000, 69% of American children lived with two parents, down from 77% in 1980. In 2000, almost a quarter (22%) of children lived with only their mothers, 4% lived with only their fathers, and 4% lived with neither of their parents. Since 1996, the percentage of children living with only one parent has not changed significantly. White, non-Hispanic children are much more likely than black children and somewhat more likely than Hispanic children to live with two parents. In 2000, 77% of white, non-Hispanic children lived with two parents, compared with 38% of black children and 65% of children of Hispanic origin. Most children spend the majority of their childhood living with two parents; however, significant proportions of children have more diverse living arrangements. Information about the presence of parents and other adults in the family, such as the parent's unmarried partner, grandparents, and other relatives, is important for understanding children's social, economic, and developmental well-being. With the diverse family structures today, the challenge is to encourage the next generation with wisdom and understanding of the purpose and function of marriage and family.

Poverty and Youth

Childhood poverty has both immediate and lasting negative effects. Children in low-income families fare less well than children in more affluent families. Compared to children living above the poverty line, children living below the poverty line are more likely to have difficulty in school, to become teen parents, and as adults to earn less and be unemployed more frequently (Duncan, Brooks-Gunn, 1997; Haveman, Wolfe, 1993). The poverty rate for children living with family members continued to decline from 18% in 1998 to 16% in 1999. The poverty rate for children has fluctuated since the early 1980's; it reached a high of 22% in 1993 and has since decreased to the lowest rate since 1979. The decrease in poverty is apparent for children living in female-headed families and is more pronounced for black children. Among black children in female-headed families, about two-thirds lived below the poverty line from 1980 to 1993, but by 1999 just over half were in poverty.

It is important to note that the poverty rate of black or Hispanic children is much higher than the poverty rate of white, non-Hispanic children. In 1999, 9% of white, non-Hispanic children lived in poverty, compared with 33% of black children and 30% Hispanic children. The full distribution of the income of children's families is important, not just the percentage in poverty. There appears to be a growing gap between rich and poor children, which suggests that poor children may experience more relative deprivation even if the percentage of poor children is declining (U.S. Census Bureau, Series P-60 various years). Regardless of the cultural ethnic background, financial strain and poverty has the potential to choke out confidence of a hopeful future. For many young people and adults alike: hope deferred makes the heart sick. We as adult leaders have a mandate to reach and teach those in impoverished communities the foundations of economic empowerment and survival skills for difficult times.

Alcohol and Drugs

Racial differences in alcohol and tobacco use are evident. Contrary to media portrayal, white teens reported the highest prevalence of daily smoking followed by Hispanics then blacks. In the year 2000, 26% of white 12th grade students reported daily smoking, compared to 16% of Hispanics and 8% blacks (Johnston, O'Malley, Bachman, 2000). In 2000, rates of heavy drinking remained largely unchanged from 1999, with 30% of 12th graders, 26% of 10th graders, and 14% of 8th graders reporting heavy drinking, i.e., having at least five drinks in a row at least once in the previous 2 weeks. Heavy drinking is more likely among Hispanic and white secondary school students than among their black counterparts. The rates are similar with illicit drug use. With white students leading, followed by Hispanics, and then black students for both 12th and 10th graders. However when reviewing the 8th grade statistics the rates were 11% for whites and blacks and 15% for Hispanics (Johnston et al., 2000). As stated with poverty the effects of drugs and alcohol on young people are the same regardless of ethnicity or social economic status. PHAT STAR curriculum encourages young people to understand the basic design of mankind and the laws of nature. Our premise is that humans have been designed to have control over the earth. For example the law of gravity places the earth under the feet of mankind. In other words when the earth (cocaine from the coca plant, alcohol fermented from grains) has control of mankind through abuse, misuse and addiction it can lead to destruction. It is important to note when things are not operating in their purposed order and design abuse is inevitable.

Violence

Violence affects the quality of life of young people throughout this nation. Youth ages 12 to 17 are twice as likely as adults to be victims of serious violent crimes, which include aggravated assault, rape, robbery (stealing by force or threat of violence), and homicide (Snyder, Sickmund, 1999). In 1999, the rate at which youth were victims of serious violent crimes were 20 crimes per 1,000 juveniles ages 12 to 17, totaling about 480,000 such crimes. Since 1993, the rate of serious violent crime against youth has decreased by 53%, down to 20 per 1,000 in 1999. Males are nearly twice as likely as females to be victims of serious violent crimes. In 1999, the serious violent crime victimization rate was 27 per 1,000 male youth, compared with 14 per 1,000 female youth. Younger teens ages 12 to 14 are as likely as older teens 15 to 17 to be victims of serious violent crimes (U.S. Department of Justice, Bureau of Justice Statistics National Crime Victimization Survey, 1999). According to reports by victims, in 1999 the serious violent juvenile crime offending rate was 26 crimes per 1,000 juveniles ages 12 to 17 years old, totaling 610,000 such crimes involving juveniles—a 50% drop from 1993 high and the lowest level recorded since the national victimization survey began in 1973.

Consequences of Premarital Sex

Data on rates of sexual activity and the age of onset has much variance. The national Youth Risk Behavior Survey (YRBS) data from the Center of Disease Control and Prevention are derived from students attending high school, and their peers who are not enrolled in school are not included, nor are middle school adolescents. For example data from an urban population in Miami, Florida, shows ages at first intercourse below the age of 12 in many adolescents, and they also reveal that as many as 24% of all 12–13-year olds have already begun to have intercourse (MMWR, 1994). The YRBS data from 1990–1997 has shown a downward trend in the percentage of adolescents in high school who have had intercourse (Mott, Fondell, Hu, 1996). Whether or not early adolescent sexual activity is linked to other adolescent risk behaviors, depends upon the population the researcher is viewing. Among African American adolescents, early sexual activity is not necessarily linked to other risk behaviors (Stanton, Romer, Ricardo, et. al, 1993). Between 1980 and 1994, the birth rate for unmarried women ages 15 to 44 increased. The birth rate for unmarried women ages 15 to 17 increased from 21 to 32 per 1,000, and the rate for unmarried women ages 18 to 19 rose from 39 to 70 per 1,000. In 1998 33% of all births were to unmarried women. Between 1994 and 1998 rates by age declined for all women under the age of 20. In 1998, the adolescent birth rate was 30 per 1,000 young women ages 15 to 17. There were 173,231 births to these young women in 1998. The 1998 rate was a record low for the Nation (Ventura, Martin, Curtain, Mathews and Park, 2000).

There are substantial racial and ethnic disparities in birth rates among adolescents ages 15 to 17. In 1998, the birth rate for this age group was 14 per 1,000 for Asians/Pacific Islanders, 18 for white, non-Hispanics, 44 for the American Indians/Alaska natives, 59 for black, non-Hispanics, and 62 for Hispanics. The birth rate for black, non-Hispanic females ages 15 to 17 dropped by nearly one-third between 1991 and 1998, essentially reversing the increase from 1986 to 1991. The birth rate for white, non-Hispanic teens declined more than one-fifth during 1991–98. In contrast, the birth rate for Hispanics in this age group did not begin to decline until after 1994; the rate fell by one-sixth from 1994 to 1998.

While nearly four-fifths of all adolescent births are first births, the steepest decline in birth rates for young teenagers in the 1990's has been for second births to adolescents who had already had one child. The pregnancy rate (sum of births, abortions, and fetal losses per 1,000) declined by one-sixth for teenagers ages 15 to 17 during 1990–96, reaching a record low of 68 per 1,000 in 1996. Rates for births, abortions, and fetal losses declined for young teenagers in the 1990's (Ventura, Mathews, Curtin, 1998).

Every year 3 million adolescents acquire Sexually Transmitted Infections (STI's). A young woman has a 1% chance of acquiring HIV, a 30% chance of getting genital herpes and a 50% chance of being infected with gonorrhea. Adolescents have higher rates of STI's than young adults. Overall many young people feel immortal, invisible and invulnerable and take risks. The danger of doing what the present desire wants is: once you satisfy the present longing the future effects are not taken into consideration. Whether a condom is used or not is not the issue here. But what is of greater concern is there is no 100% certainty that a young person participating in premarital sex will not obtain a disease, get pregnant or suffer emotional trauma. The holistic methodology of teaching toward wellness takes into consideration the physical, social, emotional, spiritual and economic ramifications of premarital sexual activity. It has been said, "There is a way of life that looks harmless. Sure those people appear to be having a good time, but all that laughter will end in heartbreak" (Proverbs 14:12, THE MESSAGE).

According to Mertz CDC 2000 report teens are high behavioral risk for acquiring STI's because they are more likely to have multiple sex partners, to engage in unprotected sex, and for young women to choose sexual partners older than themselves. Young women are biologically more susceptible to chlamydia, gonorrhea and HIV due the external position of the vaginal squamocolumnar junction. Although STD's like chlamydia, HIV and herpes are widespread across racial and ethnic groups, STD rates tend to be higher among African Americans than white Americans. Reported rates of some STI's are as much as 30 times higher for African Americans than white adolescents. There appears to be much variance in reporting of statistics in different demographic communities. Probable cause could be: African American adolescents are more likely to get health care from public clinics that report STI's more completely than private providers, the level of prevention education may vary widely across communities. In some areas community-based efforts may be widespread across social, educational, and religious organizations, but in other communities STI prevention may not be a high priority. PHAT STAR education is designed to enlighten and empower youth workers in a community with information and resources to encourage prevention education for the communities that have a high prevalence of morbidity and mortality. For example let's note chlamydia and gonorrhea.

Chlamydia

- 40% of the cases are reported among young people 15–19 years of age,
- 1999 7.2% of 15 to 24 year old females in 22 states tested positive for chlamydia,
- Prevalence is higher among minority women 15–19 years of age, 12% of African Americans, 6% Hispanics and 4% whites.

Gonorrhea

- 1997–1999 the rate among African Americans increased from 802.4 to 848.8 cases per 100,000 White slightly from 26.2–27.9 cases per 100,000 and Hispanics increased from 67.4 to 75.3 cases per 100,000 people,
- Among adolescents 15–19 years of age there was a 13% increase from 1997–1999. In 1999 the rates were slightly lower than in 1998, however the rates

among African American young men and women
remain extremely high.

The statistics reveal adolescents' expression of their sexuality can lead to negative consequences (pregnancy and STI's).
There are some factors that have been identified that influence
the onset of an adolescent's sexual debut. One example: with
girls it has been found that the more education her mother has
gone through, the later her daughter will begin to have sexual
intercourse. It is also known that girls who achieve menarche
prior to age of 12 are at greater risk for early sexual debut
(Resnick, Blum, 1994).

As adults, leaders, whether teaching our children at home,
or monitoring what they are being taught at school, should be
aware of factors which have been described among sexually active adolescents.

- Less expectation of and value in relation to achieve-
  ment,
- More tolerance of differences between themselves
  and others,
- Less religiosity,
- A greater likelihood of having friends with different
  values and views than their parents views,
- A greater influence exerted by their peers,
- Authoritarian parents,
- A greater use of alcohol and marijuana (gateway
  drugs) (Jessor & Jesor, 1975).

The challenge to us as adult leaders in to instill words of
wisdom with simplicity and relevance to the next generation.
Once the youth glean the ability to make the right choice at the
opportune time and apply it to their life they will reap the benefit of health and wellness to their soul.

Many adults are aware of the media's influence on the sexual
activity as well as other psychosocial problems. The next section will cover the impact of the media on today's adolescent
population.

Chapter 7

Media Coverage
and Its Impact

Where Are They Spending Their Time?

Every so often there would be a basketball game televised the night prior to our competition. Many members of the team would gather at someone's house and watch the game and get fired up thinking about our opportunity to get on the court. During my coaching years, I remember the night our girl's basketball team met at a player's home the night before the regional playoffs. Her mother had cooked a huge spaghetti dinner and we gathered around the TV and watched *Hoosiers* while eating desert. I was tickled, as the girls would relate scenes from the film to practice situations. Some of my players began to identify with the players in the movie, and high-five each other when they would execute a good play or score. The identification intensified as the young Indiana team in the movie wore the same color uniforms of red and gold! The next day the girls went out on the court mimicking some of the lines from the movie during warm-up and truly played at another level. They went on to win the game and move to the final four playoffs. We were one of the most unlikely teams to go that far! It was so exciting.

Positioned for the Exchange

Just as the media played an influential role in my teams life, motivating and enhancing what they already knew, there is an impact of the media today that is not always leading to a wholesome victory in the lives of young people. Data from a nationally representative sample of 2,000 students revealed the following information. The availability of media in young people's homes has increased immensely over the years. Ninety-nine percent of all American adolescents live in homes with a television; the survey indicated that the 98% of homes had a VCR and 94% a CD player. There were 82% of homes with a video game player, 74% had a cable or satellite TV, and 73% had a computer (Roberts, Foehr, Rideout, & Brodie, 1999). As early as 1999, about half of all adolescents' homes had internet access. With the exceptions of computers and internet access there were very few differences in media availability among different social classes. Computers and internet access are more common in more affluent homes; even still, half of all lower-income homes had a computer, and one-quarter of them had internet access. Most adolescents have access to many of these media in their own bedrooms. The context of which many young people participate in all forms of media is one that makes parental monitoring very difficult. Because monitoring is difficult it is important for adult youth workers to collaboratively work together instilling principles and skills of discernment into young people. When the youth we serve have their senses trained to discern. They will make wise choices pertaining to media exposure.

Television is ever-present in adolescents' homes. Nearly 70% of adolescents live in homes with three or more televisions. Two-thirds of adolescents report that the TV is on during meals. Roberts et al., study revealed television being especially pervasive in African American homes, which on average have more televisions and more televisions in adolescents' bedrooms. Adolescents total media exposure—the amount of time they spend each day using one of the mass media is extremely high. The average adolescent spends nearly seven hours each day using one or more media, this includes using different media simultaneously, for example one hour watching TV while surfing the internet was recorded as

72

one hour of media use. Among high school students, most of the time is spent watching TV (three hours per day), followed by CD's and tapes (more than an hour each day), and the radio (about an hour a day). Reading occupies far less time—about a half-hour, on average—and only about a half-hour on average—and only about one-third of high school students read more than 30 minutes each day (this includes books, magazines, and newspapers, but not homework). Usually, it has been noted that exposure to video media (TV, VCR, movies, video games) tends to follow an inverted U-shaped curve as individuals age, with more frequent use during preadolescence and adolescence than before or after. Exposure to media follows a different pattern with age, increasing linearly throughout childhood and adolescence. The time spent by today's youth engulfed in the media is quite alarming. When the television is on during meals it eliminates undistrated conversation between family members. While playing video games young people are intense to get to the next level and usually don't want to be interrupted. The video games and music have surpassed television viewing but with the music and games it can go wherever the youth go.

Reed Larson (1994) perceives one of the reasons that television viewing declines during adolescence, and listening to music increases, is that television viewing is far less satisfying to the adolescent as far as his or her developmental needs are concerned. Larson argues that television is created by adults for a general audience, where as many types of popular music are created specifically for adolescents. Studies of teenagers reveal their emotional states often feel vacant while watching television but more aroused (either positively or negatively) while listening to music (Larson, 1994; Thompson & Larson, 1995).

One thing to note from Larson's study is that television tends to link young adolescents to their families because they often watch television with other family members, whereas listening to music is often a solitary activity. The typical teenager spends 13% of waking hours in the bedroom—second only to time spent at school—and much of that time is spent listening to music (J. Brown, 1994). The hours spent in the bedroom and the increased time teens spend alone do not give them many opportunities to improve their communication skills. Could it be that as communication skills decrease that at-risk behavior will increase? Over the course of adolescence, there is a substantial increase in the amount of time adolescents spend alone, although it is greater for girls (Larson & Richards, 1991; Wong & Csikzentmihalyi, 1991). By far, the most popular television shows among teenagers are comedies, followed by dramas, movies and sports consecutively.

When it comes to music, rap and hip-hop lead the list in 1999, followed by alternative rock, hard rock or heavy metal, and country and western. There are strong ethnic differences in music preferences, with rap and hip-hop the overwhelming choices for African American and Hispanic youth. Rap and hip-hop are very popular among white youth, too, but not as popular as alternative rock.

The 1999 media usage survey discussed in the preceding pages was one of the first efforts to collect information from a representative sample of youth on their use of the internet. Not much research has been done in this area to give credibility to the role of the internet in adolescent development. From research gathered, the most frequently visited chat rooms and sites were those about entertainment (celebrities, TV shows, movies, music), sports and relationships and lifestyles (especially among older teenagers). It appears from the frequent use of websites and chat rooms about relationships that a number of teenagers are using the internet to get and give advice in many personal matters. The challenge here is whether or not the information is beneficial, or harmful.

Does the Media Really Impact the Life of a Teen?

There has been some difficulty in interpreting studies of media influence upon adolescent development. It is extremely difficult to disentangle cause from effect, because adolescents choose which mass media they are exposed to (Arnett, 1995; Arnett, Larson, & Offer, 1995). Although it has been speculated that violent film images and heavy metal music provoke aggression, it is just as likely, if not more so, that aggressive adolescents are more prone to choose to watch violent images (Arnett, 1996; Roe, 1995). There have been similar speculations reflecting sexual behavior correlation with listening to "sexy" music, but there has been very little data revealing which causes which. Casual factors has been a focus for many years. There is a place for spiritual assistance when dealing with behavioral patterns.

To the lay clergy it would be beneficial to research the mediums through which spirits gain access to the minds of the youth. Once this is identified emphasis should be on encouraging the youth to fill their minds and meditate on things true, noble, reputable, authentic, compelling and gracious (Philippians 4:8a, THE MESSAGE).

The thoughts of an individual are influenced through the somatic nervous system. Prophets of old have stated as a man thinks within his heart so shall he become. Studies have shown that arousal does take place through music. If this is so could it be that a pattern is established? If so is there a spiritual lesson to be learned? Most relevant research has focused on television as a consequence, and virtually nothing is known about impact of other media on development. Sex, violence and drugs have been given the most media impact research.

Media Violence

American media rank as the most violent in the world (Groebel, 1998; Goldstein, Sobel, Newman, 1999). In 1998, the 3-year National Television Violence Study (NTVS) concluded its examination of nearly 10,000 hours of programming on major networks, including cable and pay-per-view TV (Federman, 1998). The findings were as follows:

- The majority of shows contain violence,
- Children and adolescents view an estimated 10,000 acts of violence per year,

75

- Frequently the violence portrayed is potentially harmful, the person behind the violence is a role model,
- The violence is portrayed, as being justified and going unpunished, or the consequences are not shown,
- Guns are featured in one-fourth of all depictions,
- Fantasy violence in children's shows contained more violence than adult programming.

A recent analysis of MTV programming indicated that more than one-fifth portrayed overt violence, that one-fifth of rap videos contained violence, and weapon carrying appeared in one-quarter of all MTV videos (Strasburger & Donnerstein, 1999). Precise estimates of the most popular video games or other visual media are not available, but concerns have been raised over the impact of playing violent games on young people's behavior and attitudes. This is an area that needs more research. Exposure to violence has been linked to increased fear, heightened tolerance of violence, and greater desensitization to the effects of violence on others (Cantor, 2000). The PHAT STAR Model combines neuroscience, psychology, sociology and theology to investigate what the "Psalmist speaks of" I will set no worthless thing before my eyes.

Media and Drugs

Many analyses have shown alcohol and tobacco are pervasive in the mass media to which young people are exposed. According to one team of experts, "Alcohol, tobacco, or illicit drugs are present in 70% of prime time network dramatic programs, 38 out of 40 top-grossing movies, half of all music videos" (Strasburger & Donnerstein, 1999, pp. 129-130). Nearly 10% of the commercials that young people see on television are for beer and wine. And alcohol and tobacco companies have an increasing presence on the internet, sponsoring numerous websites and specially designed chat rooms (Strasburger & Donnerstein, 1999).

Studies that clearly reveal that exposure to messages about sex, violence and drugs causes changes in adolescent behavior are hard to find. The strongest evidence is in the area of violence, where numerous studies have shown that repeated exposure to violent imagery leads to aggressive behavior in children and youth. One important fact is that a good portion of the evidence comes from studies of aggressive behavior, rather than serious violence, and other factors, such as experiences in the family community, which is likely to have a far greater role in serious violence than does media exposure. As stated earlier there is a need for further study pertaining to the impact of media exposure and behavioral patterns of adolescents. I do believe the media is one form of exposure that is continually reinforced through repetition as well as the social surroundings of the youth.

The Media and Sex

There is a limit to the number of studies that have examined if the media can cause adolescents to have sexual intercourse at an earlier age or even influence their attitudes or beliefs about sex. However because the studies have not been done does not mean there is not an influence or impact. We know belief systems are established through a number of factors that have influence on a child's development (Irwin and Millstein, 1986). According to American Heritage Dictionary influence is a power indirectly or intangibly affecting a person or a course of events. The question PHAT STAR investigates is: what is the power or source behind media influence? According to a 1996 Kaiser Family Foundation Survey on Teens and Sex, they found the following information concerning sources of adolescents' sexual information:

- Teachers, school nurses, or classes in school: 40%,
- Media (TV, movies, or magazines): 39%,

Positioned for the Exchange

- Parents:
  36%,
- Peers:
  27%,
- Brothers, sisters, or cousins:
  12%,
- Doctors or nurses:
  9%.

The media can in fact make early sexual activity appear as normative behavior for some impressionable young teens. At the same time the media can be used to give important information about the consequences of early sexual risk-taking behavior, as well as encouraging abstinence, and sexual fidelity in marriage. Adolescents who watch a lot of music videos have more tolerant attitudes toward sexual harassment (Strouse, Goodwin, & Roscoe, 1994). The question here is what causes the attitude of tolerance? Is it because the young person has become desensitized to the value and worth of another human being? One study found that college students who frequently watched soap operas (containing high sexual content) gave higher estimates than nonviewers did of the number of real-life extramarital affairs, children born out of wedlock, and divorces. Prolonged exposure to pornography leads to exaggerated beliefs about the extent of sexual activity in the real world (Zillman, 2000).

How Do They Interpret the Media?

The interpretation of the media is where the challenge lies for most adults concerned with the next generation. The media is not simply viewed or heard—they are interpreted. Studies of violent video games, for example find that adolescents, college students, and parents rate the same games differently (Funk, Flores, Buchman, & Germann, 1999). We must realize that adolescents are not exposed to the mass media as blank slates; rather, they bring pre-existing values, beliefs, and expectations to the experience of watching or listening, and these pre-existing states influence what they perceive and remember (Leming, 1987).

It is important to note, when there are pre-existing values and beliefs in the heart and mind of a young person the media through the somatic nervous system awakens and sometimes amplifies a thought pattern. This is the danger, not knowing how to handle unhealthy patterns of thought. However this is the essence of New Testament theology. A putting off of the old and renewing the mind. As was written to a group of Romans: Embracing what God does for you is the best thing you can do for Him. Don't become so well-adjusted to your culture that you fit into it without thinking. Instead fix your attention on God. You will be changed from the inside out (Romans 12:1b–2, THE MESSAGE).

Money, Money, Money

As the adolescent population has grown throughout the years, they have become a prime target for a variety of businesses. These businesses have tapped into the fact that adolescents save less than any other age group (Fine et al., 1990; Zollo, 1999). In 1999, teenagers spent $105 billion of their own money and an additional $48 billion of their family's money (Teen Research Unlimited, 1999). Musicians today under the age of 12 emphasizing its all about the "bengies" (As in Ben Franklin whose face appears on the $100 dollar bill) or sporting platinum and gold jewelry, could very well have an influence on the minds of youth and the money of their parents. The clothing industry during this hip-hop era has capitalized on the youth market. It is important to point out the strong influence that teenagers have on each other when it comes to purchases, as well as the influence of the adolescent market extending beyond the youth as seen in the strange predictability with which adults tastes in clothing and music often follow those of teenagers, albeit in a toned-down fashion. These young people have considerable influence over their parents' purchases, which gives added incentive for advertisers to market products with the young persons taste in mind (Valkenburge, 2000).

Positioned for the Exchange

As seen in this chapter, we have reviewed how adolescents spend more time in leisure than they do in school and work combined. With this in mind, we as adult leaders have an opportunity to implement our time, treasure and talents to a generation of young people with healthy alternatives to some of the media and empower them to use their abilities to make a difference for the common good of the nation. PHAT STAR EDUCATION is designed to empower youth and those who serve them to maximize their potential and shine like stars in the universe.

~~~ Chapter 8

Prepared for the Exchange

A cross the nation there are coaches who spend extra hours in their office going over plays, or team strategy to win the ball game or conference meet. These same coaches have a good understanding of the meet or game conditions and will assign their athletes to specific tasks based on their individual potential. In any given event in track and field, the athletes go through "specificity of training" to maximize their given talent and ability. Adults involved in the life of teens bring a wealth of information from their own life story. Our role in the world is to be more than a statistic in a census report and register what occurs in life, but someone who has input into what happens. When working with adolescents in this millennium, adult youth workers cannot settle for information dissemination alone. Research reveals that some of the approaches to preventive adolescent health education involve committed adults nurturing, guiding, teaching and motivating youth, through social support systems, adult mentoring and life skills development (Dryfoos, 1994; Bronfenbrenner, 1979; Forman, Irwin & Turner, 1990). In the last few years the push to recruit mentors and volunteer leaders in the cities of America has brought forth many individuals who are willing to work with the youth. However, careful planning and organization are needed to educate and motivate with relevance and timeliness. Using the PHAT STAR Education model as a paradigm for your youth worker training may alleviate some of the time constraints of preparation for the individuals who are eager to work with the youth. The content within the curricula assists educators as well as volunteer community members with guidelines and tools to encourage at-risk youth to live a healthy lifestyle of hope and promise.

DiClemente (1996) and colleagues recommend using a comprehensive prevention approach, which is developmentally and culturally appropriate, including targeted interventions for high-risk groups, with an attached assessment. The PHAT STAR Education concept and curriculum are designed to provide an understanding of the psychological, sociological, cultural, and spiritual influences on adolescent risk behaviors. A holistic collaborative model has been designed to teach youth how to prevent and reduce risk behaviors and their adverse consequences.

As mentors and leaders we must be cognizant of the time that has been allotted to us. The writer Solomon states: "There is a time to be born and a time to die," (Ecclesiastes 3:15; NKJV). It is a fact that we will all die. Knowing this, it would be wise make the most of our today. There is an allotted time for each of us on earth, to fulfill the purpose for which we have been born. Could it be we have been entrusted to shape the hearts and minds of this generation of youth? If so, what is my responsibility? What message am I communicating and does it encourage integrity and character development? As a leader, teacher, parent, mentor or facilitator am I willing to model what I teach? For example Abraham Herschel, when referring to Jewish education, believes what is needed most is not textbooks but text-people. He believes the personality of the teacher is the text that the pupil's read, and will never forget (Herchel, 1953). This is why it is important for the instructor to have a good understanding, and see the significance of what they teach.

Teaching is both a condition and an accompaniment of discipline. To teach often means simply "to inform." In our teaching we must be aware of the ordinal laws of nature, while we nurture human nature. Too often we teach out of rote tradition rather than giving explanation and understanding to the subject matter of our teaching. Where there is understanding there is purpose! Educational reformer Paulo Freire in his book *Pedagogy of Freedom* believes that to "teach is not to transfer knowledge but create the possibilities for the production or construction of knowledge," (Freire, 1998, p. 30). Centuries ago the concept of teaching young people to be law abiding citizens was a fundamental underpinning of education, whether formal or informal. Hebrew adults were instructed to *yarah* (to cast) the children. The original idea was changed into an educational conception, since the teacher puts forth new ideas and facts as a farmer casts seed into the ground. But the process of teaching was not considered external and mechanical but internal and vital. It was important that an internal change in the student took place based on the information cast their way. In other words some things are not taught, they are caught by the influential lifestyle of the teacher. In these changing times we as adult leaders have an opportunity to give young people more than information and ideas, but to instill in them a desire to process information and acquire discernment.

Discernment actually means "to separate," to distinguish. Real learning follows genuine teaching. This word suggests a sound psychological basis for a good pedagogy. The function of teaching might be exercised with reference to the solution of difficult problems. For example King David gives us some insight when he said "Give me understanding, and I shall keep Your law; indeed, I shall observe it with my whole heart," (Psalms 119:34, NKJV). For years students have had limited opportunities to understand or make sense of topics because much of the curricula they were exposed to emphasized memory rather than understanding. This is what Alfred Whitehead (1979) would call "inert" knowledge. It embraces the mechanics of any subject—facts, procedures, and behaviors that can be acquired by memorization. It consists of information that is stored in "taxon memory systems" (O'Keefe, Nadel, 1978). The word *taxon* stems from taxonomies or lists. What is stored in this section of the brain are items that don't depend on a specific physical context. For example, many of us know how to start up a car and drive it without understanding all that is actually taking place under the hood. This comes from our routinely driving everyday.

Textbooks are filled with facts that students are expected to memorize, and most tests assess students' abilities to remember the facts. We must not exclude memorization, but understand the purpose for that which we are memorizing. Knowing the foundational functional meanings of the lists that are committed to memory enable young people to have "usable knowledge." Caine and Caine (1994) suggest, "Memorization should usually take place in the course of acquiring understanding." Young people today are in search of usable knowledge to assist them in their decision making pertaining to whole, healthy relationships and lifestyles.

The intellectual sphere of academia indicates the function of teaching to be one of illumination. Why the word illumination? If for example you were trying to keep information from your friend Robert, you would tell others that you wanted to keep him in the dark, or ignorant to the information. The service of the educator, whether parent, teacher or community youth worker is to give of illumination with instruction and admonition. For too long many of us viewed teaching as a time to instruct or deliver a didactic discourse with youth. These environments leave little room for direct personal and verbal participation. According to the National Health Education Standards (1995) there are four basic skills necessary to enhance student health literacy. They are:

1. Critical thinkers and problem solvers
2. responsible, productive citizens
3. Self-directed learners
4. effective communicators

Hopefully we can create environments for this to take place. A goal would be to introduce an interlocutory method, where there is interplay of ideas and words between young people (students) and teachers based on the knowledge received. Our challenge is to enter the classroom of life open to ideas, questions, curiosities and the inhibitions of young people.

> The teacher who really teaches, that is, who really works with contents within the context of methodological exactitude, will deny as false the hypocritical formula, "do as I say, not as I do." (Freire, 1998, p. 39)

~~⌣ Chapter 9

Awakening the Church to Community Intervention

The church is a vital part of the community, that for too long has taken a back seat to the current issues affecting the lives of teens. We have an opportunity to learn from others in the past who recognize the churches role in meeting the needs of the community. In the following section I want to encourage you to learn form others who have seen the role of the church as an integral part of meeting the needs of the community. A collaborative educational effort between the church and other community organizations can play a significant role in reaching and teaching adolescents.

The cultural factors of a community are defined as explicit and implicit guidelines that individuals "inherit" from being a part of a particular society (Helman, 1984). If a community can organize its resources effectively into a united force, it will be better able to address and resolve a community problem.

Dr. James Tyms believes that a true sense of community depends upon, and is rooted in, a God-conscious concern shared by those who make up the community. It is grounded in a people's awakened consciousness of the nature and function of the church in a changing society, rooted in the quality of relationships nurtured into existence and sustained by those who will be creative participants in the affairs of the community. Finally, a true sense of community depends upon qualitative nurture in the nurturing community that is appropriate for youth and adults who make up the given and anticipated life of the church (Tyms, 1995).

Ernest Bayles' shares his observations on the true meaning of learning within the church. He views learning as a process, or something, which must happen to people. It does not happen to school supplies or classroom furniture. But it represents a certain kind of behavior, the kind in which alterations or modifications of acts, or groups of acts, occurs (Bayles, 1950). The educational task of the nurturing community is that of inculcating the religious values and principles of a nurturing ministry as the most powerful dynamics for human development—man-making. This task can be undertaken meaningfully only when responsible agents of the church educational ministry have a clear perspective of the nurture of children, youth and adults (Tyms, 1995). The church is a community under "a new spiritual principle" set to nurture the feelings, attitudes and thoughts of individuals. This nurturing community is committed to the task of transforming human nature into something new.

For years the church in the African American community emerged in the social context of slavery. The message of becoming a "new creature" was amplified during a dehumanizing social order of injustice, oppression, brutality and the denial of human rights. In spite of all the dehumanizing experiences endured by African Americans, the church continued to grow. In an oppressive and hostile social order, African American men and women were exploited in the labor market, dealt with unjustly in the legal system and reduced to a status of non-persons in the sociocultural world. Viewing the church as a community of refuge, E. Franklin Frazier felt that for the slave who worked and suffered in an alien world, religion offered means of catharsis for their pent-up emotions and frustrations. Moreover, it turned their minds from the suffering and privations of this world to a world of comfort and peace and the weary would find rest for their souls (Frazier, 1984). The book of Isaiah speaks to individuals whose minds can be at peace when they are going through trouble. Our nation was called to pray and seek God during the greatest crisis seen in America September 11, 2001. The power of prayer is often encouraged to those seeking peace of mind and persevere through difficult times (Isaiah 26:3, NKJV).

Dealing with Injustice

Even with the injustices that are evident in the juvenile justice system and special education placements, the church can play a role of comfort, solace and more importantly, empowerment and education. The words of Jesus Himself, "Learn of Me, Go ye therefore and teach every nation," (Matthew 11:28, 28:18–19, NKJV) speak to the potential to learn, and that all people (nations-*ethnos*) are to be taught. Youth workers in the church have an opportunity to encourage self-awareness and true identity to teens.

Not a One Man Job

Edward P. Wimberly, in his book *Pastoral Care in the Black Church*, notes the fact that holding to the Black church tradition has not been the function of the pastor alone. The sustaining dimension of Black pastoral care has been the function of the total church acting as a caring community (Wimberly, 1979). Traditionally Black churches in rural settings had a pastor on the scene once a month, and twice during a three-month period or less. In this situation, the cohesive, sustaining and caring function of the church was in the hands of the laity. They kept alive the sharing, caring and sustaining function of the church in prayer meetings, the Sunday school and young people's organizations. An invisible church, forbidden to gather for prayer, steals away to pray for freedom, human dignity and healing. The visible Black church has made the invisible church a powerful force as a cohesive, sustaining and caring community throughout history.

With ability to identify the transforming power of "All mighty" God, through affirmations of a just and loving God, we can have a reverence for all human beings. The God of righteousness and liberation becomes our own and is passed on to our children and grandchildren. The church has an opportunity to appropriate its serving arm in this hour to a generation who may be struggling with what the future holds.

Edward Wimberly (1979) pointedly described comprehensively the role of the church past and present, as one of sustaining, guiding, healing, reconciling, nurturing, witnessing, parenting and caring. The pastor can once again be seen as being God's shepherd among the people in their care, facilitating and working together with the total congregation to sustain persons in crisis.

We all can learn lessons from Carter G. Woodson who believed that from the days of slavery to the present, the Black church has performed the role of sponsoring the cause of education among African American people. The preacher aided by the congregation validates the assumption that African American people can develop intellectually. Carter G. Woodson emphasized that few persons believed that the Negro was capable of the mental development known to the white man (Woodson, 1921). The challenge to them then was to show that their race has the possibilities in the intellectual world, and to bring forth proof to uproot the argument that one race is inferior to other people. To make the challenge more concrete, Woodson addressed the issue of the day, and that was, can the Negro master grammar, language, and literature of Latin and Greek? (Woodson, 1921) This was the heart of Jesus who stated that whoever took upon His yoke to learn from Him could learn, and what is known to many as the great commission re-emphasized this though in the statement "Go and teach all nations—ethnos." The Black church was a vehicle used for years to educate as well as a means of bringing the minister and people to a higher level of thought. In many instances, leaders in the church have not always been up front leading the people toward the goals of liberation, freedom, education, person-hood and people-hood. Often the clergy have specialized in emotionalizing the people, and not empowering them. Although Woodson's writings were directed to a certain people in the 1920's the principals are Biblical and work with every people group on earth. It is not a "Black thing" it is a "God thing." If God and His Word (the Bible) are one, then what works for one people group should work for another because God shows no partiality. "It's God's own truth nothing could be plainer: God plays no favorites! It makes no difference who you are or where you're from" (Acts 10:34, THE MESSAGE).

Clarity from the Spirit of God

Karl Jaspers has logistically drawn a contrast between the conforming and reorganizing or restructuring aspects of education, depending on the qualitative nature of the cultural world. He believes that man can become more decisively himself in proportion to the clarity and richness of the world with which his own reality becomes united (Japers, 1951). It appears that if the substance of the whole becomes unstable, questionable and degenerate, education becomes insecure and disintegrated. When confusion and disquiet prevail in society, adults and adolescents are left with a sense of void and discontent. In frustration the advocates of religious education are challenged to turn to the nurturing ministry of education with the hope that the coming generation may be guided to determine most effectively what the moral and spiritual quality of the world must become.

Tyms (1995) believes the genius of the Christian faith, under girded by a sound philosophy of education and creative affirmations about human nature, and committed to the business of religious nurture, is perennially focused upon the progressive reconstruction of man's inner and outer world. The book of 2 Peter speaks to the fact that God through His divine power has given us everything pertaining to life and godliness through the true knowledge of Him (2 Peter 1:3 NKJV). George Albert Coe (1917) believed that education aims at the progressive reconstruction of society. He characterizes the revolutionary thrust of religious education, suggesting that there is a differentiating quality in education, inherent in the disposition to selected parts of the cultural world for preservation. With a genuine interest

in human persons, thus, the church through its spiritual challenges and values obligates man to place values—economic and
intrinsic with human personality—at the apex of the value scale.
The church has a divine window of opportunity to walk in
its purpose of being as a lighthouse to the community like never
before.

> The church needs a new and greater generation of men of
> good will. With strong character sufficient for the task of world
> leadership; so needed today to save our civilization from de-
> struction toward which she seems to be headed, finer men
> and women capable of living happy useful lives. (Ernest Li-
> gon, 1948 pp. 10–18)

George Brock Chisholm (1957) in his book *Prescription for Survival* says:

> The church needs a now generation of emerging youth who
> shall be able to look critically and analytically at some of the
> characteristic certainties, inherent in the ways of the older
> generation. (p. 27)

James Baldwin (1961) spoke to the church and the state
about sizing up the situation of youth almost forty years ago
that has current relevance.

> We, therefore, all of us have a grave responsibility to these
> young people. Our failure, now, to rise to the challenge they
> represent can only result in the most unimaginable demoral-
> ization among them, and among their children. I would rather
> not think of the probable effects on such demoralization of
> the life on this country and on the role we play in the West-
> ern World. (p. 25)

The passion behind the PHAT STAR intervention is to educate and empower the youth workers so they can empower the
youth who have been entrusted to their care. I believe there are
functions that the church can fulfill that the school cannot, and

there is a role that public education plays for those who cannot afford private school education. The challenge for the school administrators is to recognize that there are some issues that the school teachers or guidance councilors cannot meet, and that is to speak to the spirit of a young person. Spiritual battles take spiritual weapons. There have been numerous situations on school campuses where the psychologist and sociologist did not have the answers. We must be willing as a collaborative group leading and empowering the next generation to recognize when we must give the baton to a colleague who has been prepared in areas where we lack. It is only our pride and arrogance that would say we have all the answers. We must allow individuals who have crossed the sphere of influence of a young person's life, to do what they have been appointed to do in the very hour of connectedness. Oh that we would realize we all look through a glass dimly. We need the gifts that lie in another individual that could very well assist in saving the life of a young person.

Chapter 10

The School Educator and Parent Collaboration

Just as the church is challenged to meet the needs of young people, parents, and educators must work together in a fresh new way. If the young person is to be viewed in a holistic manner, there are some things academically that the parent might not have a grip on, and must trust the expertise of the school educator. When it comes to issues of moral character and behavior, the school educator and administration needs to work closely with the parents. The challenge here is for the parent to do whatever it takes to stay involved in the schooling of their child. I would encourage the educator to indicate respect for the parent's knowledge and understanding of their child, even if you perceive they may not understand. It is important for the educator to give the parent an opportunity to speak and be heard. The role of the parent and or guardian is to let their desires be made known in a manner that is respectful and honoring of the educator's skills and abilities. To the educator, be mindful that when you give advice and suggestions, the person may or may not choose to implement them.

Parental support is associated with better adolescent adjustment during school transitions. In any transition there is a need for clear communication. Generally speaking, parents are the most influential persons in a child's life. If at all possible try to stay connected to the school. It is more beneficial to be physically present at school to gain information than get a phone call or note. There are some benefits to your involvement. When you are involved you can provide knowledge about your child that can influence what and how he or she is taught. Your knowledge of your child's educational program will ensure school-to-home continuity so that many skills can be reinforced. Your involvement will increase expectation for your child and could result in academic and social gains. There is also a safeguard that is developed so that the needs of your child are discussed and met by the school system.

In many cases and school systems parents often feel overwhelmed by the amount of information they are provided and the technical terms used. For example, new teachers particularly, when they first meet parents or address them at a group meeting, rely on familiar cliché's or terms such as norms, developmental needs, heterogeneous grouping, cognitive skills, higher-order thinking, which may mean little to some parents. It is important to be sure you are communicating with clarity. There are times individuals tend to patronize parents, especially those from lower income districts. One thing to remember is that you are both on a team with a common goal, the young person's success.

Both the teacher and parent need to become aware of their own feelings of defensiveness. If these feelings are too strong to be put aside, postpone your meeting until any tone of aggressive defensiveness has subsided. It is very important for the school educator and community youth worker to focus on the needs and interests of parents and their child and not on their values. However, the parent's values must be taken into consideration. One example would be when dealing with the sex education issue and educating a child concerning abstinence until marriage. Let's take this concern a little deeper.

This has been an issue that many have argued about for years, however I believe if we would get honest and be willing to educate young people about this issue, and not just dispense knowledge, the young people would make healthy choices pertaining to this area of their life. Many problems in education have stemmed from the fact that meaningfulness is disregarded or misunderstood. Too often we as educators and parents have given our children the quick mechanical packaged answer to some of life's complex issues because it takes time to explain—and trust to believe that our child is willing to, or has the capability to, process through to what we perceive the correct answer should be. It is very important that a young person begin to develop their own convictions about the issues of life based on the values and information that have been learned throughout their life.

Meaningfulness is disregarded in many ways. For example, many outcomes are spelled out in purely behavioral terms that emphasize memory and ignore meaningfulness for the learner. It may be an objective—for example, the student will be able to define and recognize the most common STIs and label the male and female reproductive organs. The knowledge embodied in these outcomes constitutes the mechanics of a subject. Both, declarative knowledge (knowing that something is the case) and procedural knowledge (knowing how to do something) can be what is called surface knowledge if all that is required is programming and memorization. We must go beyond the notion that learning is determined by preconceived outcomes. As already mentioned, even discovery learning is often a guise for having students arrive at predigested understandings. This is why it is important for us to know what the young people have been digesting pertaining to this area of sexuality.

Meaningfulness learning, on the other hand, is essentially creative. All students must be given permission to transcend the insights of their teachers. Insight is much more important in education than is memorization. Felt meaning begins as an unarticulated general sense of relationship and culminates in the "aha" experience that accompanies insight. Once an adolescent has been given information and is allowed to discuss what they understand from the information we are giving them they have an opportunity to gain true understanding. They are now positioned to make a wise and healthy decision. For example we would discuss the female anatomy and dialogue about the etymology of word *hymen* (meaning marriage) which is the thin layer of tissue covering the birth canal. The following are sample questions that could be asked: Why do you suppose the thin layer of tissue covering the vagina opening is called the *hymen*? And . . . Now that you understand the meaning of *hymen*, who do you suppose should be crossing the birth canal?

This will give the student an opportunity to process through an answer rather than memorizing a fact for a test. The processing allows for them to be able to use the information at another time. For example when they are pressured in a relationship to have sexual relations before marriage, they will be reminded of what they have learned and hopefully they will make the wise decision based on previous knowledge. It could be because they were allowed to process information there is a connection. Now, the decision to abstain is made because they realize they are not married to the individual that is pressing the issue of having sex.

It is crucial that with such a sensitive subject there be educated faculty who have studied not only the curriculum, but have found ways to encourage discussion and understanding based on scientific evidence and not their own perception of what to teach. Research supports the fact that the younger an individual is the more susceptible they are to disease. We as educators have a mandate to teach the whole truth and not just our opinionated ideas. We have an opportunity as parents, educators, clergy and community center directors to collaborate and be of like mind to educate, empower and enlighten the youth to lives of wholeness and health.

The "STAR" Model

The "STAR" Model is the base foundation of PHAT STAR EDUCATION. This model introduces the holistic concept of PHAT STAR training and curriculum. Biblical integration is also introduced as the participants learn the star model.

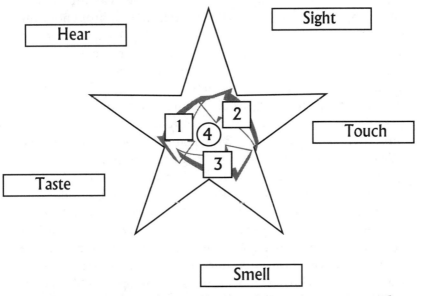

1 = the "mind", 2 = the "will", 3 = the "emotions", 4 = the "spirit"

This is viewed as the body, soul and spirit principle. We are spirits, we have a soul and we live in a body, to shine like a star here on earth.

Positioned for the Exchange

The model illustrates the five senses being the gateway to the mind of the adolescent. A brief overview of the organization of the nervous system is discussed, the emphasis being the sensory division (five senses), the central nervous system and motor division. The philosophy in the training is to view how thoughts and actions enter the mind through the senses of an individual. For example behavior patterns such as drinking, smoking, anger or rage tend to develop after there has been an initial entrance through the gateway of the senses. This could come about through something said or done to an individual, early childhood trauma or surroundings, being what they have seen, heard or felt (physically or emotionally).

With a vision to work with local churches and para-church organizations, our community workshops introduce the concept of "Biblical integration." The phrase "Biblical integration" coined by Kenneth Gangel (1987) is referred to throughout the workshop. It is essential that each of the participants understand the influence they have on every child they come in contact with. Many times Christian leaders forget that God has commanded each of us to develop our mind. "Love the Lord your God with all your heart and with all your soul and with all your mind" (Matthew 22:37). The word heart is translated *kardia*, representing the part of our living being that pumps oxygenated blood throughout the body. Soul is translated *psuche* where we get the English word psychology. This represents our feelings and emotions, which interlink with the last word, mind. Mind is translated *dianoia*, which refers to the deep understanding and knowledge of an individual. The integrative principle is discussed to better understand how and why adolescents make healthy behavior decisions. According to Gangel, there are at least three steps involved in learning how to apply biblical integration. They are: 1. Know the scriptures intimately, 2. Study the culture diligently, and 3. Analyze events and issues theologically.

The next important concept communicated in the PHAT STAR curricula is the order of nature and human life. A detailed explanation of how destruction becomes inevitable when things are not in line with their original design (For example if I take the plant from its source, the soil, and do not place it back, it will die). It is imperative that all the participants understand the terminology pertaining to prevention. Time is given to discuss the differences between primary, secondary and tertiary preventive measures pertaining to sexual behavior, drug and alcohol abuse, violence or any other psychosocial disorder. The three levels of prevention are taught from a biblical perspective of strongholds. Primary prevention is viewed as what can be taught to the child to prevent negative behavior patterns from ever being established. With secondary prevention "How do I change this pattern, and get the help necessary to be well again" is discussed. Tertiary is viewed as, who can help me walk, or carry my stretcher, as I feel crippled in this area of my life? If I am to live with the repercussions of where I am, who will walk with me in the area that I limp? The emphasis being that of communicating effectively these modes of prevention to the young people and the adults they will be collaborating with, at home, church, or in their organization.

Every session of training and curricula is integrated with the biopsychosocial concept (Irwin, Millstein, 1986) and now theological perspective of adolescent development. As the youth workers learn scientific terminology with biblical presuppositions, the concepts are easier to comprehend. For example, while learning terms such as *pathogen* the youth workers viewed two parallel lines diagramming a path that a person might walk on, then we discussed the prefix "o" meaning without or away from, and "gen" coming from the root word *genesis* meaning beginning. A textbook definition of a pathogen is discussed while dialoguing about things that can move us off our path of health we could or should be walking in. Here the adult youth worker is learning ways to assimilate their biblical understanding with the terminology needed to communicate effectively to the young people entrusted to their charge. I believe it is important for those who would teach the PHAT STAR philosophy they first be grounded in it themselves. Therefore continuing to teach what they themselves have become convinced of.

Positioned for the Exchange

Informed adult Christians are indispensable to the challenge of translating Christian values and attitudes into social, political, educational and economic institutions (Cooke, 1976). It appears that one of the keys to Christianity's future is community; but essential to modern-day communities are competent, well-trained adults who live out their context of faith and experience (Cooke, 1976, Simmons 1976, 1978).

The PHAT STAR curriculum encourages the youth workers to approach issues facing today's young person with the star model. Each point on the star represents one of our five senses. This is where sensory neurons take impulses to the brain. Time is spent in the explanation of the star model of how impulses are carried to and from the brain and affect our body's actions and reactions. The focus however is upon the mind, will and emotions (the *soul*, or seat of one's personality). Every impulse prior to going to the brain is processed through the somatic nervous system. Youth workers are encouraged to view the behavioral patterns and causal factors of at-risk behavior patterns from a holistic (spirit, soul and body) perspective.

To bring clarity to this way of thinking, an explanation of what is perceived as spiritual *warfare* is discussed. This concept is introduced by using the term learned in the foundation of the training, *pathogen*. We use a visual slide of the neurological pathway of what someone sees or hears, and how it is biologically processed into an action. We pay attention to what may have entered the pathway of the senses of a young person that may cause certain behavior patterns. Another way of viewing this is to investigate what has interrupted an individual's path of origin to wellness? The five senses are viewed as the gates to the mind. It is understood that sometimes people have had illegal entrance, through what others have said, and done to them, (physical abuse, sexual abuse, verbal, etc.). These issues are addressed and discussed in small groups as they worked out certain fictitious scenarios. As stated in the definitions, a stronghold is a way of thinking that has been so cultivated in a person's life it is now what comes natural or has become a habit pattern. Another term used for this word stronghold is a *fortress*. It usually occurs when an individual feels so strongly about some-thing that he or she builds a fortress or defense around his or her belief. The hope is that youth workers will better under-stand spiritual strongholds and abusive addictive patterns. The Apostle Paul admonishes the Christian "For though we walk in the flesh (*body, five senses*), we do not war according to the flesh, for the weapons of our warfare are not of the flesh but divinely powerful for the destruction of fortresses. We are destroying speculations and every lofty thing raised up against the knowl-edge of God, and we are taking every thought captive to the obedience of Christ," (2 Corinthians 10:3–5, NASB). This verse speaks to the battleground, through words like speculations, knowledge and thoughts. All of these words have to do with the mind. Therefore as adult youth workers we must beware of our own cultural biases, "just say no" cliché's and scare tactics, real-izing they may not be the best way to encourage young people in the art of reasoning and refusal skills. A collaborative educa-tional effort between the church and other community organi-zations can play a significant role in reaching and teaching today's youth. Dr. James Tyms (1995) believes that a true sense of com-munity depends upon, and is rooted in, a God-conscious con-cern, shared by those who make up the community. It is grounded in a people's awakened consciousness of the nature and func-tion of the church in a changing society, rooted in the quality of relationships nurtured into existence and sustained by those who will be creative participants in the affairs of the community. We have an opportunity to be those creative participants created in the image of God, to fulfill His purposes in the earth. Let's run this race with endurance and see it to its end!

～ Chapter 12

A Welcomed Witness
"What Has Been Said"

At any track meet, or ball game, there are people in the stands who are shouting and cheering for those in the game or participating in an event. If you are a spectator, you will hear others talking about their perception of how the game is being played. However, those who actually played have much to say about how the game was played. As the New England Patriots captured the World Championship Title, the post game interviews were worth waiting for. We got to hear the heart of those who were on the field, the hands on folks! So what did it take to win? How do you feel your training prepared you for the competition? What advice would you give to a young person wanting to reach this same plateau? These are questions athletes might be asked, as spectators await their response. The following statements are from those who have participated in the PHAT STAR EDUCATION training in their response to how the training has impacted them. Hopefully you will be encouraged and challenged to look into the PHAT STAR EDUCATION program yourself.

Positioned for the Exchange

"I was very encouraged by the workshop. I believe the program should be fully developed throughout churches and schools for more clarity of information. From all that I grasped, it was wonderful, thought provoking and study inducing."

"The greatest gift of the workshop was the fact that all my previous knowledge and experience of at-risk youth prevention has now become wrapped up in the Bible with a spiritual core. It also confirmed the vision of our ministry, to truly make a difference in the lives of a small group of kids over an extended period of time. They will later impact their peers."

"The workshop was very informative and spiritually inspiring. It has motivated me to use this knowledge in teaching the youth. As for myself, I was encouraged and challenged to share what I've learned with those whom I encounter. I am accountable for what I've learned here."

"I realized my need to tie everything together, the social, spiritual, physical and emotional. I also learned some spiritual concepts, and practical ways I can get them across to my kids! Thank you!"

"The workshop was interesting, empowering and liberating. Excellent!!!"

"I learned that everything could be taught alongside the Bible. For so long I have heard about all the preventive measures of drug and alcohol abuse and sexual abstinence until marriage and the Bible and spiritual things. But I have never heard the two concepts merged together. I also learned that kids could handle this information no matter how complex if it is taught in a developmental relevant way."

"This workshop was good! I learned about how social behavior is both physical and spiritual. I also learned different ways to learn about how to reach people of different cultures and socioeconomic backgrounds. It was almost like an overview of my introduction to Psychology and Neurology class."

"This workshop helped me to contexualize and make the Word of God relevant to today's issues. Speaking and addressing the physical, social, and emotional components of an adolescents life was taught in a manner that anyone could grasp it. I was able to put together thoughts and theories of adding a spiritual lifestyle to my approach to the ministry that I am involved with. This was more than training it was the development of thinking different—systems thinking, a renewing of the mind."

"There were good concepts to use with any group of people. I was given a better understanding of Genesis the beginning of things, and God's order and plan for all. The concept of holistic ministry has 'opened my eyes' regarding youth ministry. I have an understanding now, that I must look at the whole person— spirit, soul and body. I must be willing to investigate the underlying issues."

"I am not currently involved in a youth program, but I have two teenagers and my home is where all the youth of the neighborhood nest. I know God wants to use me. I just have to submit. I have learned some concepts that I need to apply to my life before I can address anyone else with them. The workshop has taught me to be steadfast in the Bible. Participating in this workshop was like being born-again, again! I gained new insight and revelation as to how I can share truth with the young people."

"This workshop was truly a blessing. It has helped me to see the big picture and to look at things not only with the natural eye, but with the spirit."

"I really appreciated how you taught us the definitions of words such as pathogen and disease using biblical principles to draw out the meaning. When we looked at primary, tertiary and secondary prevention in light of spiritual strongholds in ones life I truly caught the meaning of the word. I never really looked at teaching and understanding in such a holistic way. The understanding of becoming a 'living epistle known and read by men' is where I want to be. I like how it was stated that God has the answers to everything pertaining to life and godliness."

"The cultural piece was excellent and very helpful. I am doing a lot of cross-cultural work, and what I learned about the history of the city and the migration north of African-Americans was awesome. I never knew all that took place in light of the economic strain that many in the inner city were under, and why. Viewing some of the behavioral patterns that manifest in the inner cities of America, and ways in which people develop dangerous coping patterns was enlightening to me. Having been in this workshop I have learned to intercede before I interject!"

"This was by far the best workshop I have ever sat through. Every session was powerful and meaningful. I am very glad I attended."

"Thank you for getting through the entire workshop material. The information was very practical. I wish we had a little more time for questions and interaction. That which we did was great it just seemed we needed more time. The information that was coming forth encouraged most of us in the room to talk through the realities that we saw in our own lives. The meal times and breaks all we could talk about were the concepts we had learned and the fresh insight that came forth. As individuals shared in the workshop about how the development piece made sense it opened a flood gate for so many of us. I am blown away with the knowledge and empowering that happened with this workshop. Areas where I've felt defeated I now know I have the victory."

"The at-risk information was fascinating. The information was taught in a way I could understand, not just with my mind, but also with my spirit and heart. The facilitator was a great teacher and encourager."

"The workshop reminded me that our battle is a spiritual one. Rather than being upset with the youth themselves, we need to wage battle against the spirits that have strongholds in their lives."

"These sessions helped me with many things I had been dealing with. I now realize that the kids need education (especially sex ed.). Being a nurse, I see a desperate need for this education. I loved the way the facilitator taught the underlying issues. What impacted me greatly was how the facilitator illustrated why kids may feel the way they do."

"I can't begin to find appropriate words to express what God is stirring-up in side of me . . . The sessions have rekindled my desire to work with the youth in my group. As a leader, I must take heed to the times—create an environment where they can learn to hear God for themselves."

"The workshop sessions were meaningful, challenging, needed, worthwhile and helped increase my thirst for more knowledge."

With all that has been said, we are still growing and learning. It is essential to learn throughout life.

Take Your Place and Finish the Race

We are living in a day and time when America is on guard and called to be sober and vigilant. The evildoers of the recent terrorist attack have threatened to attack again which keeps us on our guard. If the young people of our nation are to live a life of wholesome peace and joy, we must be positioned to reassure them that it will take a generation of people who are willing to grow in wisdom and stature, having favor with God and with man.

Can we as adult leaders stress the importance of wisdom and character being instilled in the next generation? PHAT STAR

Positioned for the Exchange

EDUCATION and Dr. René Rochester are committed to doing all that it takes to empower and encourage the next generation and those who serve them with relevant tools to run this race of life to win!

A Note to Those Positioned to Receive!

To the youth of this nation, I believe you are in a position to make a radical difference in the future of America as well as the world. In the next few years my challenge to you is to learn all you can learn concerning how to walk in wisdom and understanding. Take time to understand the basic makeup of mankind. We live in an imperfect world with imperfect people. The Bible states with clarity that as time progresses on the earth, lawlessness will increase and the love of many will grow cold. Take time to read and reason with those not only of governmental knowledge, but with those who understand spiritual matters. May you hold fast to the Truth that has become real to you, and position yourself to **receive** the baton, and run the race set forth before you with endurance!

> Do you not know that those who run in a race all run, but only one receives the prize? Run in such a way that you may win it. (1 Corinthians 9:24, NASB)

⁓ Bibliography

Arnett, J. (1996). *Metalheads*. Boulder, CO.: Westview Press.

Arnett, J. (1995). Adolescents' use of media for self-socialization. *Journal of Youth and Adolescence*, 24, 519–533.

Banks, J. A. (1997) *Educating Citizens in a Multicultural Society*, Teachers College, Columbia University.

Banks, J. A. & Banks, C. A. M. (ed.). (1995). *Handbook of Research on Multicultural Education*. New York: Macmillan.

Banks, J. A. (1991) *Teaching Strategies for Ethnic Studies* (5ᵗʰ ed.) Boston: Allyn & Bacon.

Barber, B. (1994). Cultural, family, and personal contexts of parent-adolescent conflict. *Journal of Marriage and the Family*, 56, 375–386

Baron, R. M., Tom, D., & Cooper, H. M. (1985). Social Class, race and teacher expectations. In J. Dusek (ed.), *Teacher Expectancies*. Hillsdale, NJ: Erlbaum.

Baratz, S. S. & Baratz, J. C. (1970). Early Childhood Intervention: The Social Science Base of Institutional Racism. *Harvard Educational Review*, 40 (1), 29–50.

Baumrind, D. (1991). The influence of parenting style on adolescent competence and substance abuse. *Journal of Early Adolescence*, 11, 56–95.

Baumrind, D. (1978). Parental Disciplinary patterns and social competence in children. *Youth and Society*, 9, 239–276.

Bayles, Ernest, (1950). *The Theory and Practice of Teaching*. New York: Harper & Brothers.

Bender, H. W., and Darkenwald, G. G. Differences Between Teaching Adults and Pre-Adults: Some Propositions and Findings. *Adult Education*, 1982, 33 (3), 142–155.

Berry, F. Light, *Color and Environment*. New York: Van Nostrand Reinhold, 1969.

Botvin, G. J. (1986). Substance abuse prevention research: Recent developments and future directions. *Journal of School Health*, 56, 369–374.

Bowers, R. D. "Testing the Validity of the Andragogical Theory of Education in Selected Situations." Unpublished doctoral dissertation, Boston University, 1977.

Brindis, C., Irwin, C. E. Jr., & Milstein, S. G. (1992). United States Profile: The Demography of Adolescents. In E. McAnarney, R. Kreipe, D. P. Orr, & G. Commerci (ed.), *Textbook of Adolescent Medicine* (pp. 12–27). Philadelphia: W. B. Saunders.

Bronfenbrenner, U. (1979). *The Ecology of Human Development*. Cambridge, MA: Harvard University Press.

Brophy, J. E., & Good, T. L. (1970). Teachers' communications of differential expectations for children's classroom performance: Some behavioral data. *Journal of Educational Psychology*, 61, 365–374.

Brown, B. (1999). "You're going out with who?": Peer group influences on adolescent romantic relationships. In W. Furman, B. Brown, & C. Feiring (ed.). (1999). *Contemporary Perspectives on Adolescent Romantic Relationships* (pp. 291–329). New York: Cambridge University Press.

Brown, B., Mory, M., & Kinney, D. (1994). Casting crowds in a relational perspective: Caricature, channel, & context. In R. Montemayor, G. Adams, & T. Gullotta (ed.). *Advances in Adolescent Development, Vol. 5: Personal Relationships During Adolescence*. Newbury Park, CA: Sage.

Brown, B. (1990). Peer groups and peer culture. In S. S. Feldman & G. R. Elliot (ed.), *At the Threshold: The Developing Adolescent* (pp. 171–196). Cambridge, MA: Harvard University Press.

Caine, R, Caine, G. (1994) *Making Connections: Teaching and The Human Brain*, Addison-Wesley Publishing Company.

Cantor, J. (2000). Media violence. *Journal of Adolescent Health*, 27, 30–34.

Carnegie Council (1997) *Great Transitions: Preparing Adolescents for a New Century*, Carnegie Corporation of New York

Cheren, M. I. "Facilitating the Transition from External Direction in Learning to Greater Self-Direction in Learning in Educational Institutions: A Case Study in Individualized Open System Postsecondary Education." Unpublished doctoral dissertation, School of Education, University of Massachusetts, 1978.

Coe, Albert George, (1917). *A Social Theory of Religious Education*. New York: Charles Scribner's Cons.

Conant, J. (1959). *The American High School Today*. New York: McGraw-Hill

Cooke, B. J. (1976) *Ministry to Word and Sacraments: History and Theology*. Philadelphia: Fortress Press.

Cooper, H., & Good, T. (1983). *Pygmalion Grows Up: Studies in the Expectation Communication Process*, New York: Longman.

Cox, Harvey. (1984). *Religion in the Secular City: Toward a Postmodern Theology*, New York: Simon and Schuster.

Denning, J. & Verschelden, C. (1993). Using the focus group in assessing training needs: Empowering child welfare workers. *Child Welfare*, 6 (72), 569–579.

DiClemente, R., Hansen, N., Ponton, E. *Handbook of Adolescent Health Risk Behavior* New York: Plenum Press 1996.

Doll, W. E., Jr. (1993). *A Post-modern Perspective on Curriculum*. New York: Teachers College Press.

Donovan, J. E. & Jessor, R. (1985). Structure of problem behavior in adolescence and young adulthood. *Journal of Consulting and Clinical Psychology*, 53, 890–904.

Dryfoos, J. G. (1997) in *Enhancing Children's Wellness: The Prevalence of Problem Behaviors*: Implications for Programs, 17–46.

Dryfoos, J. G. (1994). *Full Service Schools: A Revolution in Health and Social Services for Children, Youth and Families,* San Francisco, CA.

Dryfoos, J. (1993). Schools as places for health, mental health, and social services. *Teachers Colleger Record*, 94, 540–567.

Dryfoos, J. G. (1990). *Adolescents At-risk.* Oxford: Oxford University Press.

Dreyfuss, G. O., Cistone, P. J., & Divita, C., Jr. (1992). Restructuring in a large district: Dade County, Florida. In Carl D. Glickman (ed.). *Supervision in Transition,* (pp. 43–51). Alexandria, VA: ASCD Press.

Duncan, G. & Brooks-Gunn, J. (ed.). (1997). *Consequences of Growing Up Poor*. New York, NY: Russell Sage Press.

Duncan, G. (1994). Families and neighbors as sources of disadvantage in the schooling decisions of white and black adolescents. *American Journal of Education*, 103, 20–53.

Dusek, J. B., & Joseph, G. (1985). The bases of teacher expectancies. In J. Dusek (ed.), *Teacher Expectancies*. Hillside, NJ: Erlbaum.

Edelman, P., & Ladner, J. (ed.). (1991). *Adolescence and Poverty: Challenge for the 90s*. Washington, DC: Center for National Policy Press

Ensminger, M., Lamkin, R., Jacobson, N. (1996). School leaving: A longitudinal perspective including neighborhood effects. *Child Development*, 67, 2400–2416.

Federman, J. (ed.): National Television Violence Study, Vol. 3. Thousand Oaks, CA.: Sage, 1998.

Fine, G., Mortimer, J., & Roberts, D. (1990). Leisure, work, and the mass media. In S. Feldman & G. Elliott (ed.), *At the Threshold: The Developing Adolescent*. (pp. 225–252). Cambridge, MA: Harvard University Press.

Flewelling, R. L., & Bauman, K. E. (1990). Family structure as a predictor of initial substance use and sexual intercourse in early adolescence. *Journal of Marriage and Family*, 52, 171–181

Fordham, C., & Ogbu, J. (1986). Black students' school success: Coping with the burden of "acting white." *Urban Review*, 18, 176–206

Forman, S., Irwin, C. E. Jr., & Turner, R. (1990). *Family structure, emotional distancing and risk-taking behavior in adolescents*. Pediatric Research, 27, 5A

Fraizier, E., F., (1984) *The Negro Church in America*, New York: Schocken Books

Freire, P. *Pedagogy of Freedom*, Rowan & Littlefield Publishers, Inc. 1998

Freire, P. (1971). *Conscientizing as a way of liberating*. Liberation (March). A. T. Hennelly (ed.), 1990. Maryknoll, NY: Orbis.

Freire, P. *Pedagogy of the Oppressed*. New York: Seabury Press, 1970.

Funk, J., Flores, G. Buchman, D., & German, J. (1999). *Rating electronic games: Violence is in the eye of the beholder*, Youth and Society, 30, 283–312.

Gaines, Ernest J. (1993). *A Lesson Before Dying*, New York: Alfred A. Knopf.

Gangel, K., (1987). *Thinking like a Christian: An Evangelical analysis of Rationality*. Christian Education Journal, Vol. 3, No. 1, Scripture Press Ministries.

Garbarino, J. (1992). *Children and Families in the Social Environment* (2nd ed.). Hawthorne, NY: Aldine.

Positioned for the Exchange

Gay, G. (1994). *At the Essence of Learning: Multicultural Education.* West Lafayette, IN: Kappa Delta Pi.

Gecas, V., & Seff, M. (1990). *Families and adolescents: A review of the 1980's.* Journal of Marriage and the Family, 52, 941–958.

Good T. (1987). *Two decades of research on teacher expectations: Findings and future directions.* Journal of Teacher Education, 38 (4), 32–47.

Goldstein A. O., Sobel R. A., Newman G. R.: *Tobacco and alcohol use in G-rated children's animated films.* JAMA 281:1131–1136, 1999.

Gou, G. (1998). *The timing of the influences of cumulative poverty on children's cognitive ability and achievement.* Social Forces, 77, 257–287.

Griffin, David Ray, Cobb, John B., Jr., Ford, Marcus P., Gunter, Pete A.Y., & Ochs, Peter. (1993). Founders of Constructive Postmodern Philosophy: Peirce, James, Bergson, Whitehead, and Hartshorne. Albany: State University of New York Press.

Griffin, D. R., (1988a) *The Reenchantment of Science: Postmodern Proposals.* Albany: State University of New York Press.

Griffin, D. R., (1988b) *Spirituality and Society: Postmodern Visions.* Albany: State University of New York Press.

Groebel J: *The UNESCO Global Study on Media Violence.* In Carlsson U, von Feilitzen C (ed.): *Children and Media Violence.* Goteborg, Sweden, UNESCO International Clearinghouse on Children and Violence on the Screen, 1998, pp 181–199.

Hayes, C. D., *Risking the Future: Adolescent Sexuality and Child Bearing.* Vol. 1 Washington, D.C. Academy Press, 1987.

Hertherington, E. M., Henderson, S., & Reiss, D. (1999). Adolescent siblings in stepfamilies: Family functioning and adolescent adjustment, *Monographs of the Society for Research in Child Development*, 64, Serial No. 259.

Helman, C. (1984). *Culture, Health and Illness: An Introduction For Health Professions.* Bristol, Eng.: John Wright & Sons, Stonebridge Press.

Bibliography

Heschell, A., J., *The Spirit of Jewish Education.* Jewish Education 24/2 Fall, 1953/:19.

Hollins, E. R., King, J. E., and Hayman, W. C. (ed.). (1994). *Teaching Diverse Populations: Formulating a Knowledge Base.* Albany, NY: SUNY Press.

Irwin, Charles E. (1987). *Adolescent Social Behavior and Health*, San Francisco: Jossey-Bass.

Irwin, C. E., Jr., & Millstein, S. G. (1986). *Biophychosocial correlates of risk-taking behaviors during adolescence: Can the physician intervene?* Journal of Adolescent Health Care, 7, (Suppl), 82S–96S.

James, S., Heller, D., & Ellis, W. (1992). *Peer assistance in a small district:* Windham, Southeast, Vermont. In Carl D. Glickman (ed.), Supervision in Transition (pp. 43–61). Alexandria, VA: ASCD Press.

Jasper, Karl, (1951). *Man in the Modern Age: Garden City:* Doubleday and Co.

Jessor, R., Chase, F. Jessor, S. L., & Donovan, J. E. (1983). *Time of first intercourse: A prospective study.* Journal of Personality and Social Psychology, 44, 608–626.

Jessor, R., & Jessor, S. L. (1977). *Problem Behavior and Psychological Development:* A Longitudinal Study of Youth. New York: Academic Press.

Johnston, L. D., O'Malley, P. M., & Bachman, J. G. (1999)(2000) National Survey Results on Drug Use from the Monitoring of Future Society.

Johnston, L. D., O'Malley, P. M., & Bachman, J. G. (1994) National Survey Results on Drug Use From the Monitoring the Future Society, 1975–1992 (NIH Publication #93-35 97). Rockville, MD. National Institute on Drug Abuse. U.S. Department of Health and Human Services, Public Health Service, National Institutes of Health.

Kaplan, H. B., Johnson, R. J., & Baily, C. A. (1987). *Deviant peers and deviant behaviors. Further elaboration of a model.* Social Psychology Quarterly, 50, 277–284.

117

Positioned for the Exchange

Kaplan, H. B. (1980). *Deviant Behavior in Defense of Self.* New York: Academic Press.

Kliebard, Herbert. M. (1986). *The Struggle for the American Curriculum*: 1893–1958. Boston: Routledge and Kegan Paul.

Knowles, M. S. *The Adult Learner: A Neglected Species.* (3rd ed.) Houston: Gulf, 1984. (Originally published in 1973; 2nd ed. 1978.)

Kupersmidt, J., Burchinal, M., Leff, S., & Patterson, C. (1992, March). A longitudinal study of perceived support and conflict with parents from middle childhood through adolescence. Paper presented at the biennial meetings of the Society for Research on Adolescence, Washington.

Ladson-Billings, G. (1992). *Liberatory Consequences of Literacy: A Case of Culturally Relevant Instruction for African American Students.* The Journal of Negro Education, 61(3), 378–391.

Ladson-Billings, G. (1994). *The Dreamkeepers: Successful Teachers of African American Children.* San Francisco: Josey-Bass.

Larson, R., Verma, S. (1999). *How children and adolescents spend time across the world: Work, play, and development opportunities.* Psychological Bulletin, 125, 701–736.

Larson, R., & Richards, M. (1994b). *Family emotions: Do young adolescents and their parents experience the same states?* Journal of Research on Adolescence,4, 567–583.

Larson, R., & Richards, M. (1991). *Daily companionship in late childhood and early adolescence: Changing development contexts.* Child Development, 62, 284–300.

Leming, J. (1987). *Rock music and the socialization of moral values in early adolescence.* Youth and Society, 18, 363–383.

Leventhal, H., & Brooks-Gunn, J. (2000). *The neighborhoods they live in: The effects of neighborhood residence on child and adolescent outcomes.* Psychological Bulletin, 126, 309–317.

Lincoln, Yvonna S. (1992). *Curriculum studies and the traditions of inquiry*: The humanistic tradition. In Philip W. Jackson (ed.), Handbook of research on curriculum (pp. 79–98). New York: Macmillan.

Bibliography

Lindeman, Eduard C. *The Meaning of Adult Education*. New York: New Republic, 1926.

Maccoby, E., & Martin, J. (1983). *Socialization in the content of the family: Parent-child interaction*. In E. M. Hertherington (ed.), Handbook of Child Psychology: Socialization, Personality, and Social Development (Vol. 4). pp. 1–101. New York: Wiley.

McCord, J. (1990). *Problem Behaviors*. In S. S. Feldman & G. R. Elliott (ed.), At the Threshold: The Developing Adolescent (pp 414–430). Cambridge, MA: Harvard University Press.

McLaren, Peter, & Dantley, Michael. (1990). *Leadership and a critical pedagogy of race*: Cornel West, Stuart Hall, and the prophetic tradition. Journal of Negro Education, (1), pp. 29–44.

McLoyd, V. C., Jayaratne, T. E., Ceballo, R., & Borquez, J. (1994). *Unemployment and work interruption among African American mothers: Effects on parenting and adolescent socioemotional functioning*. Child Development, 65, 562–589.

Minkler, M., & Wallerstein, N. (1997a). *Improving health through community organization and community building*. In K. Glanz, F.M. Lewis, & B.K. Rimer (ed.), Health Behavior and Health Education: Theory, Research, and Practice (2nd ed., pp. 241–269). San Francisco: Jossey-Bass

Monttemayor, R. (1984). *Maternal employment and adolescents' relations with parents, siblings, and peers*. Journal of Youth and Adolescence, 13, 543–557.

Montemayor, R., (1983). *Parents and adolescents in conflict: All families some of the time and some families most of the time*. Journal of Early Adolescence, 3, 83–103.

Mory, M. (1992, March). *Love the Ones You're with: Conflict and Consensus in Adolescent Peer Group Stereotypes*. Paper presented at the biennial meetings of the Society for Research on Adolescence, Washington.

Mosher, W. D., & McNally, J. W. (1991). *Contraceptive use at first premarital intercourse*: United States, 1965–85 Family Planning Perspectives, 23, 108–128.

Positioned for the Exchange

Mott F. l., Fondell M. N., PN. et al: *The determinants of first sex by age 14 in a high-risk adolescent population*. Family Planning Perspective, 28:13, 1996.

National Research Council. (1993). *Losing Generations*. Washington, DC: National Academy Press.

O'Keefe, J., and L. Nadel (1978). *The Hippocampus as a Cognitive Map*. Oxford: Claredon Press.

Oliver, D. W., & Gershman, K. W., (1989) *Education, Modernity, and Fractured Meaning: Toward a Process Theory of Teaching and Learning*. Albany: State University of New York Press.

Osgood, D. W. , Johnston, L. D., O'Malley, P. M. & Ingersoll, G. M. (1989). *Reported sexual behaviors and self-esteem among young adolescents*. American Sociological Review, 53, 81–93.

Osajima, Keith. (1992) *Speaking silence*. JCT: An Interdisciplinary Journal of Curriculum Studies, 9 (4), pp. 89–96.

Paschall, M. J., & Hubbard, M. L. (1998). *Effects of neighborhood and family stressors on African American male adolescents' self-worth and propensity for violent behavior*. Journal of Consulting and Clinical Psychology, 66(5), 825–831.

Paster, V. S. (1985). *Adapting psychotherapy for the depressed, unacculturated, acting-out, Black male adolescent*. Psychotherapy, 22, 408–417.

Patriarca, L. A., & Kragt, D. M. (1986). *Teacher expectations and student achievement: The ghost of Christmas future*. Curriculum Review, May / June, 48–50.

Payne, R. S. (1994). *The relationship between teachers' beliefs and sense of efficacy and their significance to urban LSES minority students*. Journal of Negro Education, 63 (2), 181–196.

Penland, P. *Individual Self-Planned Learning in America*. Washington, D. C.: Office of Education, U. S. Department of Health, Education, and Welfare, 1977.

Peters, J. M., and Gordon, S. G. (1974). *Adult Learning Projects: A Study of Adult Learning in Urban and Rural Tennessee.* Knoxville: University of Tennessee.

Phenix, P. (1975). *Transcendence and the curriculum.* In William F. Pinar (ed.), *Curriculum Theorizing: The Reconceptualists* (pp. 323–337). Berkley, CA: McCutchan.

Phillips, D. A. (1991). *With a little help: Children in poverty and child care.* In A. Huston (ed.), *Children in Poverty: Child Development and Public Policy.* (pp. 158–189). New York: Cambridge University Press.

Pinar, William F., (1988b). *Time, place and voice: Curriculum theory and the historical moment.* In William F Pinar (ed.), *Contemporary Curriculum Discourses* (pp. 264–278). Scottsdale, AZ: Gorsuch, Scarisbrick.

President's Science Advisory Committee. (1974). *Youth: Transition to Adulthood. Chicago:* University of Chicago Press.

Purpel, David E. (1989). *The moral and spiritual crisis in education: A Curriculum for Justice and Compassion in Education.* New York: Bergin and Garvey.

Ravitch, D. (ed.). (2000). Brookings Papers on Education Policy. Washington, DC: Brookings Institution.

Resnick, M., & Blum, R. (1994). *The association of consensual sexual intercourse during childhood with adolescent health risk and behaviors.* Pediatrics, 94, 907–913.

Roberts, D., Foehr, U., Rideout, V., & Brodie, M. (1999). *Kids and Media @The New Millennium.* Menlo Park, CA: Kaiser Family Foundation.

Rochester, R. D. (1999). *Design Implementation and Evaluation of the PHAT STAR WORKSHOP* dissertation for The University of Texas at Austin

Roe, K. (1995). *Adolescents' use of socially disvalued media: Towards a theory of media delinquency.* Journal of Youth and Adolescence, 24, 617–631.

Rosenthal, R., & Jacobson, L. (1968). *Pygmalion in the Classroom: Teacher Expectation and Student Intellectual Development*. New York: Holt, Rinehart & Winston.

Ruether, Rosemary R. (1983a). *Sexism and God-talk: Toward a Feminist Theology*. Boston: Beacon Press.

Seidman, E., Yoshikawa, H., Roberts, A., Chesir-Teran, D., Allen, L., Friedman, J. L., & Aber, J. L., (1998). *Structural and experiential neighborhood contexts, development stage, and antisocial behavior among urban adolescents in poverty*. Development and Psychopathlogy, 10, 259–281.

Sells & Blum (1996) *In Handbook of Adolescent Health Risk Behavior* edited by DiClemente, R., Hansen, W., Ponton, L. Plenum Press, New York, 1996, p. 29.

Sharma, A., McGue, M., & Benson, P. (1998). *The psychological adjustment of United States adopted adolescents and their nonadopted siblings*. Child Development, 69, 791–802.

Shea, Christine, Kahane, Ernst, & Sola, Peter. (1989). *The New Servants of Power: A Critique of the 1980's School Reform Movement*. New York: Greenwood Press.

Simmons, H. C. (1978) *Building Maps for the Journey of the Middle Years*. The Living Light, 15 (3), 337–347.

Simmons, H. C. (1976). *Human Development: Some Condition as for Adult Faith at Age Thirty*. Religious Education, 71(6), 563–572

Simons, R., Johnson, C., Beaman, J., Conger, R., & Whitebeck, L. (1996). *Parents and peer group as mediators of the effect of community structure on adolescent problem behavior*. American Journal of Community Psychology, 24, 145–171.

Slattery, P., (1992b). *Theological dimension of the school curriculum*. Journal of Religion & Public Education, 19 (2–3), p.p. 173–184

Smetana, J., & Gaines, C. 1999). *Adolescent-parent conflict in middle-class African-American families*. Child Development, 70, 1447–1463.

Smetana, J. (1994). *Morality in context: Abstracts, applications, and ambiguities.* In R. Vasta (ed.), Annals of Child Development (Vol. 10, pp. 83–130). London: Jessica Kingsley.

Smetana, J. (1989). *Adolescents' and parents' reasoning about actual family conflict.* Child Development, 59, 1052–1067.

Smetana, J. (1988a). *Adolescents' and parents conceptions of paternal authority.* Child Development, 59, 321–335.

Smetana, J. (1988b). *Concepts of self and social convention: Adolescents' and parents reasoning about hypothetical and actual family conflicts.* In M. Gunnar & W. Collins (ed.), Minnesota Symposium on Child Psychology (Vol. 21, pp. 79–122). Hillsdale, NJ: Erlbaum.

Smith, David G. (1988). *Experimental eidetics as a way of entering curriculum language from the ground up.* In William F. Pinar (ed.), Contemporary Curriculum Discourses (pp.417–436). Scottsdale, AZ.: Gorsuch, Scarisbrick

Snyder, H. N. and Sickmund, M. (1999). *Juvenile Offenders and Victims: 1999 National Report* (Publication No. NCJ 178257, p. 26). Washington DC: Office of Juvenile Justice and Delinquency Prevention.

Spindler, G. and Spindler, L. (1993). *The Process of culture and Person: Cultural Therapy and Culturally Diverse Schools.* In P. Phelan and A.L. Davidson (ed.). *Renegotiating Cultural Diversity in American Schools* (pp. 27–51). New York: Teachers College Press.

Stanton, B., Romer, D., Ricardo, I., et al: *Early initiation of sex and its lack of association with risk behaviors among adolescent African-Americans.* Pediatrics 92: 13–19, 1993.

Strasburger, V. C., Donnerstein, E.: *Children, adolescents, and the media: Issues and solutions.* Pediatrics 103: 129–139, 1999.

Steinberg, L. (2001). *We know some things: Adolescent-parent relationships in retrospect and prospect.* Journal of Research on Adolescence, 11, 1–20.

Strouse, J., Goodwin, M., & Roscoe, B. (1994). *Correlates of attitudes toward sexual harassment among early adolescents.* Sex Roles, 31, 559–577.

Positioned for the Exchange

Thompson, R., & Larson, R. (19950. *Social context and the subjective experience of different types of rock music.* Journal of Youth and Adolescence, 24, 731–744.

Tough, A. M. (1982) *Intentional Changes: A Fresh Approach to Helping People Change.* Toronto: Ontario Institute for Studies in Education.

Tough, A. M. (1979) *The Adult's Learning Projects.* (2nd ed.) Toronto: Ontario Institute for Studies in Education. (Originally published 1971.)

Tough, A. M. (1967). *Learning Without a Teacher.* Toronto: Ontario Institute for Studies in Education.

Troyna, B., & Hatcher, R. (1992). *Racism in Children's Lives: A Study of Mainly-White Primary Schools.* London and New York: Routledge.

Tyms, James, (1995). *The Black Church as a Nurturing Community,* St. Louis: Hodale Press.

U.S. Bureau of the Census. (1999a). Current Population Survey, March 1999. Washington, DC: U.S. Department of Commerce.

Births: Final data for 1998. National Vital Statistics Reports, 48 (3). Hyattsville, MD: National Center for Health Statistics.

Ventura, S. J., Mathews, T. J., and Curtin, S. C. (1998). Declines in teenage birth rates, 1991–97: National and State patterns. National Vital Statistics Reports, 47 (12). Hyattsville, MD: National Center for Health Statistics.

Ventura, S. J., Mathews, T. J., and Curtin, S. C. (2000). Declines in teenage birth rates, 1991–97: National and State patterns. National Vital Statistics Reports, 47 (12). Hyattsville, MD: National Center for Health Statistics.

Ventura, S. J. (1995). *Births to unmarried mothers*: United States, 1980–92. Vital Statistics Reports, 53 (Series 21). Hyattsville, MD: National Center for Health Statistics.

Wallerstein, N. B., & Sanchez-Merki, V. (1994). *Freirian praxis in health education*: Research results from an adolescent prevention program. Health Education Research: Theory and Practice, 9, 105–118.

Weis, Lois. (1983). *Schooling and cultural production: A comparison of black and white lived culture.* In Michael Apple & Lois Weis, *Ideology and Practice in Schooling,* (pp. 235–261).

Weis, Lois, (1988). *Class, Race, and Gender in American Education.* Albany: State University of New York Press.

Werner, E., & Smith, R. (1982). *Vulnerable But Invincible: A Longitudinal Study of Resilient Children.* New York: McGraw-Hill.

Whitson, A., L. (1991). *Constitution and Curriculum.* London: Falmer.

Whitehead, A. N. (1979). *Process and Reality.* New York: The Free Press

Wimberly, Edward, P. (1979). *Pastoral Care in the Black Church.* Nashville: The Abingdon Press

Wineburg, S. S. (1987). *The self-fulfillment of the self-fulfilling prophecy.* Educational Researcher, 16 (9), 28–37.

Wong, M., & Csikszentmihalyi, M. (1991). *Affiliation motivation and daily experience: Some issues on gender differences.* Journal of Personality and Social Psychology, 60, 154–164.

Woodson, Carter, (1921). *History of the Negro Church in America.* Washington, DC: The Associated Press.

Yau, J., & Simetana, J. (1996) *Adolescent-parent conflict among Chinese adolescents in Hong Kong.* Child Development, 67, 1262–1275.

Zemke, R. and Zemke, S. (1995). *Adult Learning: What do we know for sure?* Training, 6 (32), 31–40.

Zemke, R. and Zemke, S. (1981). *30 things we know for sure about adult learning.* Training, 6 (18), 45–52.

Zillman, D. (2000). *Influence of unrestrained access to erotica on adolescents' and young adults' dispositions toward sexuality.* Journal of Adolescent Health, 27, 41–44.

Zollo. (1999) *Wise Up to Teens: Insights into Marketing and Advertising to Teenagers* (2nd ed.) Ithaca, NY. New Strategist

Zuckerman, M., Ball, S. & Black, J. (1990). *Influences of sensation seeking, gender, risk appraisal, and situational motivation on smoking.* Addictive Behaviors, 15, 209–220.

Zuckerman, M. (1979). *Sensation seeking: Beyond the Optimal Level of Arousal.* Hillsdale, NJ: Erlbaum.

Zuckerman, M., Eysenck, S., & Eysenck, H. I. (1978). *Sensation seeking in England and America: Cross-cultural, age, and sex comparisons.* Journal of Consulting and Clinical Psychology, 46, 139–149.

To order additional copies of

Positioned *for the* Exchange
Who Will *Impact* the Next Generation?

Have your credit card ready and call

Toll free: (877) 421-READ (7323)

or send $20.00* each plus $4.95 S&H**

to
WinePress Publishing
PO Box 428
Enumclaw, WA 98022

*Washington residents please add 8.4% tax.
**Add $1.00 S&H for each additional book ordered.